D0603700

DISCARD

PEOPLE AT ODDS

ISRAEL AND THE ARAB WORLD

PEOPLE AT ODDS

PEOPLE AT ODDS

ISRAEL AND THE ARAB WORLD

Heather Lehr Wagner

Chelsea House Publishers
Philadelphia

CHELSEA HOUSE PUBLISHERS

EDITOR IN CHIEF Sally Cheney
DIRECTOR OF PRODUCTION Kim Shinners
CREATIVE MANAGER Takeshi Takahashi
MANUFACTURING MANAGER Diann Grasse

Staff for **ISRAEL AND THE ARAB WORLD**

ASSISTANT EDITOR Susan Naab
PICTURE RESEARCHER Sarah Bloom
PRODUCTION ASSISTANT Jaimie Winkler
SERIES AND COVER DESIGNER Keith Trego
LAYOUT 21st Century Publishing and Communications, Inc.

http://www.chelseahouse.com

3 5 7 9 8 6 4 2

Library of Congress Cataloging-in-Publication Data

Wagner, Heather Lehr.
  Israel and the Arab world / Heather Wagner.
    p. cm. — (People at odds)
Summary: Outlines the history of the Arab-Israeli conflict over the founding
of the state of Israel, from 1948 to 2001.
  ISBN 0-7910-6705-X
  1. Arab-Israeli conflict—Juvenile literature. [1. Arab-Israeli conflict.
2. Palestine—History—20th century. 3. Israel—History—20th century.]
I. Title. II. Series.
DS119.7 .W285 2002
956.9405—dc21
                                                              2001007937

CONTENTS

1

The Promised Land

ate in the afternoon of May 14, 1948, a festive group of members of the Jewish People's Council gathered at the Tel Aviv Museum. The Council consisted of representatives from the Jewish community in Palestine and the Zionist movement, and they were celebrating as the final hours of British occupation of the region drew to a close.

Britain had ruled the territory of Palestine since 1917, following the defeat of the Ottoman army and the collapse of the Ottoman Empire. But in the aftermath of World War II, Britain found itself unable to police all of the flashpoints in its empire. India and Ireland were in chaos, London had been fiercely bombed in the Blitz, and the continuous battles between Arabs and Jewish settlers

Shown here is the region of the world called the "Middle East." Many countries in the Middle East have long been a source of contention within the area as well as outside of it. In this book, you will learn more about the conflicts in Israel, an important area in the Middle East, and the Arab world surrounding it.

The Western Wall, sometimes called the "Wailing Wall," holds great significance for Jews and Palestinians alike. For it is on this site that Jews believe King Solomon erected a temple that housed the two tablets of the Ten Commandments; and it is on this same site that Arabs believe the Prophet Muhammad received the word of God through the angel Gabriel, which he recorded in the Arabic language in the Koran.

in Palestine left British politicians despairing of a solution.

By May of 1947, Britain had given up. Turning to the United Nations to help it determine the best way to manage the region, the British representative to the UN General Assembly noted, "Having failed so far, we now bring it to the United Nations in the hope that it can succeed where we have not." And the UN did resolve the matter, influenced heavily by pressure from the United States: slightly more than 55 percent of Palestine was granted to Jewish settlers to form a Jewish state, resulting in a situation where more than half of the territory was given to less than 30 percent of the population. Hundreds of thousands of Arabs would find themselves on the Jewish side of the divided territory when Britain evacuated on May 14, 1948.

But for the Jewish People's Council, gathered on the eve of their Sabbath within the halls of the Tel Aviv Museum, it was a time for celebration, as their long-held dream of a Jewish state was about to become a reality. Their leader was David Ben-Gurion, a 62-year-old immigrant from Poland, whose earliest memories consisted of learning Hebrew on his grandfather's lap and listening to his father speak about *Eretz Israel*, the Land of Israel known as Palestine.

Ben-Gurion had focused on this land, spoken of with hushed reverence by his family, and had worked actively for it since the age of 14, when he and two friends founded a club designed to promote the study of Hebrew and emigration to Palestine. Six years later, he would emigrate himself, sailing on a Russian ship in August of 1906 toward Palestine. His earliest experience with the Arabs that populated the region was quite intimate. When the ship docked on September 7, Arab workers quickly climbed up the side of the boat and, as was the custom for porters there, lifted up both passengers and luggage, depositing them into small boats that then ferried them to shore.

But the fate of the Arabs who had literally carried him to the shores of Palestine was of little significance to Ben-Gurion as he toasted the birth of a new Jewish state on that afternoon. Standing before the jubilant crowd, Ben-Gurion noted the history that had brought them to that place, the spiritual and political forces that had shaped their identity dating back to Biblical times, concluding with the stirring declaration of "the establishment of a Jewish state in Eretz-Israel, to be known as the state of Israel."

This Declaration of Independence went on to outline the

On the left, the new prime minister of Israel, David Ben-Gurion, signs a document proclaiming the new "Jewish state in Eretz-Israel, be known as the state of Israel" in 1948 in Tel Aviv. With him are the foreign minister of Israel, Moshe Shertok (to the right of Ben-Gurion), and an unidentified man in the center. The new state of Israel was formed out of 55% of Palestine, which was given up by Britain after years of rule, and awarded to Jewish settlers of Palestine by the United Nations.

guidelines that would form the essence of the new nation. In addition to establishing the state of Israel, it called for Jewish immigration, for the "Ingathering of Exiles." It established the provisional government, noted that a constitution would be formed within the next several months, and asserted the right of Jewish people to govern themselves. It also called for peace and cooperation with the Arabs of Israel and neighboring Arab nations in a common effort to promote the advancement of the entire Middle East.

The peace that the document promised would prove short-lived. As the Jewish community in Palestine celebrated its Declaration of Independence, as the new state was officially recognized by the U.S. government, and as the British prepared to evacuate the territory, the armies of five Arab nations—Egypt, Iraq, Jordan, Lebanon, and Syria—massed on the border. They would invade Palestine the very next day.

THE CONFLICT BEGINS

For the Israelis, the war that began on May 15, 1948, was a war for independence. In their eyes, the establishment of the state of Israel was not something that had taken place on that single day in May, but rather the natural culmination of a series of events that dictated the need for a restoration of what most Jews viewed as their homeland. As the horrors of the Holocaust unfolded, and the full extent of what the Jewish people had suffered gradually came to light in the aftermath of World War II, public outrage demanded some sort of restitution. Many nations had turned their backs when European Jews sought refuge from the Nazi regime; now some of these same nations argued vigorously for the right of the Jewish people to create their own safe haven, a homeland in the Middle East.

Were the motives of these nations based on a need to make amends? The answer is not so simple. Humanitarian intentions were joined by strategic and political moves, certainly on the part of the evacuating British (who believed that a Jewish state might be more friendly to Western interests than an Arab one) and the Americans (who were eager to establish a friendly partner in the Middle East).

The Arab inhabitants of the region (whose population in the territory of Palestine was nearly double that of the Jews) were horrified at what they viewed as the arbitrary and unequal aspects of the borders that had been drawn by the UN, which turned over huge sections of Arab-inhabited land to the Jews. They were angered at the seizure of their land by people they viewed as Western immigrants, rather

This picture shows a parade to an anti-Nazi protest in New York City in May of 1933. Part of the historical influence on the Jewish people's drive to create a Jewish homeland was the extermination of Jews during World War II in Europe.

than native sons and daughters returning to their homeland.

For the land of Palestine was not simply an empty and arid desert, "a land without people awaiting a people without a land," as some writing of that time suggested. Instead it was a settled land, dotted with vast farms and vibrant towns, a land with citizens who had cultivated its earth for centuries. Families who had lived in a region for many generations were suddenly confronted with the prospect of being forced from their homes to make way for a new group of settlers who called this land their "homeland," because their ancestors had lived there in Biblical times.

These Arabs did not view themselves as Palestinians, but rather felt their strongest ties to the nations of Syria and Lebanon. Much of the land in northern Palestine belonged to wealthy landlords living in Beirut or Damascus, who allowed the local families to live on their property in exchange for farming the land. Should the land be allotted to the new nation of Israel, these local tenants would lose both their homes and their livelihoods.

The neighboring Arab nations felt a strong responsibility to ensure that their interests in the region were protected, that their land was secured, and that the promises of an independent Arab nation made by the British at the time of occupation were honored. With the memories of their own independence still fresh, each Arab nation knew the importance of guaranteeing that Arab land could not be seized and turned over to Western interests at the whim of the United Nations or any other international body.

So it was that both sides came to battle convinced of the justness of their cause, and willing to fight to the death, if need be, to protect their homeland. David Ben-Gurion, the newly elected prime minister of the new state of Israel, took to the airwaves to broadcast a message to his nation on the day that the war began. His words would prove prophetic: "Something unique occurred yesterday in Israel, and only future generations will be able to evaluate the full historical significance of the event." The war would last no more than a year. But the battles between Israelis and Arabs continue to this day.

The war was at is fiercest in the early months, as members of the five nations making up the Arab coalition moved into

Palestine from four flashpoints. The Lebanese army invaded from the north; the Syrian army from the northeast. Israel was engaged in battle with the Iraqi army and the army of the Arab Legion (representing Jordan) on its eastern front, while the Egyptian army swept up into Palestine from the south. In the regions around the cities of Nazareth and Jerusalem, the invading armies were joined by local Arab forces.

While the Arab armies succeeded in the earliest days of the war, it quickly became clear that they were outnumbered both in men and weapons. Their activities were frequently uncoordinated, and the success they might have enjoyed had they worked together quickly faded as each army sought its own aims during battles. At critical points in the war, such as during Israel's attempt to end the siege of Jerusalem, the lack of unity and effective communication among the Arab forces proved too great a weakness. After several truces had been declared and then broken, armistice agreements were finally signed, first with Egypt, then with Lebanon, Jordan, and ultimately Syria. Iraqi forces withdrew from the territory of Israel. By the end of the war, an additional 2,000 square miles had been occupied by Israeli troops—territory in the Galilee, the Negev Desert, the area around Jerusalem, and the West Bank. But these agreements, while ending the war, did not formally recognize the state of Israel nor permanently settle the issue of boundaries. Five wars and countless acts of violence and terrorism later, the same questions would still haunt the region.

For the Arabs of Palestine, the war and its aftermath resulted in a massive evacuation. Nearly 800,000 Arabs fled their homes, including most of the wealthy and well educated. Those that stayed were principally farmers and the poor. Many of those who chose to remain in Israel were unable to return to their homes. For Palestinians, the events that followed the war are known as the *Nakhba,* or disaster.

In May of 1948, soon after the state of Israel was proclaimed, five Arab nations from the Middle East—Egypt, Iraq, Jordan, Lebanon, and Syria—invaded Israel to protect the interests of the Arab people of Palestine who had been dispossessed by the U.N.'s land grant to Jewish settlers. Shown here are Arab refugees leaving the Galilee region of an area that was formerly Palestine to go to Lebanon where there was no fighting, in November of 1948. Nearly 800,000 Arabs fled their homes before and after the war.

But for David Ben-Gurion, the end of the war meant a new focus on shaping the state of Israel. He laid out bold plans to encourage immigration of Jews to Israel, to draft women into the army, to settle this new land being carved out of the desert. He would succeed in many of his plans for creating a strong military power out of this newborn nation. But each step forward that Israel took brought greater conflict with its Arab neighbors. The land was central to the hearts and hopes of both the Jewish and Arab peoples. Their promised land would bring great sorrow to both sides.

2

Shaping a Nation

In the aftermath of the first Arab-Israeli war, the territory initially granted to Israel had extended considerably into land intended to be part of an Arab state. In armistice agreements held by the United Nations, Israel was granted the right to continue to occupy the land it had seized during the war (some 2,000 square miles). The territory of Palestine was further divided among its Arab neighbors, with 140 square miles in the Gaza Strip given to Egypt and 2,270 square miles in eastern Palestine (later known as the West Bank) and East Jerusalem going to Jordan (known at the time as Transjordan). The vast majority of the territory (some 8,300 square miles) was given to Israel.

The region became dotted with borders. The city of Jerusalem was divided between Israeli and Jordanian territory. Demilitarized zones sprang up in the north, between Israel and Syria, and on the border between Egypt and Israel, as well as two within the city of Jerusalem itself. Each of these would become the site of disputes, and ultimately armed conflict.

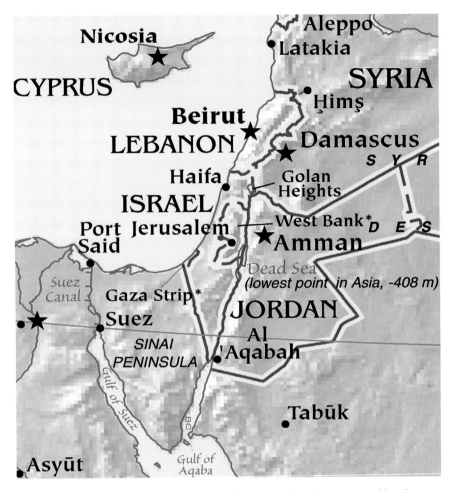

This is a map of Israel, although it is not the original territory granted by the United Nations. Israel as we know it today is composed of the original territory from Palestine awarded to Jewish settlers, plus territory won in wars with neighboring Arab nations.

The hopeful plan was that these armistice agreements would ultimately and rapidly lead to peace treaties. But another 30 years would pass before even one peace treaty would be signed, that between Egypt and Israel.

The loss of Palestinian territory was a humiliating blow to most Arabs. Refugees streamed into neighboring countries, creating a humanitarian crisis as social services were stretched. The Arabs believed that their cause was clear and just, and resentment against the West and its intervention on behalf of Israel was high.

Arab leaders who had participated in the war would also pay the price for defeat. The nationalism—the demand for Arab rights—that spread after the war would topple several Arab leaders in its wake. The Egyptian monarchy would soon fall, leaders in Syria and Lebanon would be assassinated, the king of Jordan would be shot, and a revolution would overthrow the government of Iraq.

The Israeli response to Arab outrage was to dig in deeper. By 1950, the capital of Israel was moved from Tel Aviv to Jerusalem, a clear sign that Israel had no intention of ever relinquishing any territory gained as a result of war. Hundreds of thousands of Jewish immigrants from Europe, Asia, and North Africa poured into the region, further straining resources. These new immigrants would need to be fed, housed, educated and given jobs. Many of them were directed into the former Arab territories to build new settlements.

And David Ben-Gurion, in his dual roles as prime minister and minister of defense, began the process of shaping Israel's armed forces into one of the most dominant military powers in the region. Diplomatic relations were cemented with the United States and the Soviet Union. Israel joined the United Nations. A new nation was being built, but its future would not be easy or peaceful.

A DEFEATED ARMY FINDS ITS FOCUS

The defeated Arab nations all suffered in the aftermath of the 1948 war with Israel, but Egypt found itself in a particularly perilous position as the post-war era began. Egypt's possession of the Gaza Strip was significant, but did little to

This portrait of King Farouk I, the king of Egypt from 1937 to 1952, is from the beginning of his reign. Farouk tried to reestablish control of Egypt after the Arab loss in the war with Israel by attacking Great Britain. One of his military officers staged a revolution during Egypt's conflict with Great Britain, and Farouk was deposed from his throne in 1952.

comfort a nation struggling with the dual crises of a budget deficit and a humiliated and desperate army.

A stronger and wiser leader might have been able to bring the country back from this loss, but the king of Egypt, King Farouk, was not that man. His government was widely criticized as corrupt and backward, and at a time when the vast majority of Egyptians struggled under crippling poverty, the indulgent lifestyles of Egypt's ruling class inevitably sparked great resentment. Worse still, King Farouk's roots dated back to a line of royals who were neither Egyptian nor Arab. The lower classes, the students, the intellectuals, militant Islamic groups and army officers slowly began to come together, a motley group united by their common distaste for the monarchy.

Three years after Egypt's defeat at the hands of an Israeli army, King Farouk tried to reestablish control and draw the country together by striking out against a much bigger target: Great Britain. The trouble began with anti-British rallies and riots in the towns of Ismailia and Port Said along the Suez Canal, where Britain had bases. British troops patrolling the Canal were the target of frequent terrorist attacks, and Farouk's government was unable or unwilling to put a stop to the violence.

The trouble escalated until January 25, 1952, when Britain ordered all armed Egyptians, including Egyptian police, out of the town of Ismailia. Farouk's order to the police was clear: resist the British. As a result, some 50 Egyptian policemen were killed, and riots soon spread to Cairo.

Egypt was quickly engulfed in civil unrest and violence. With a stable military, Farouk might have been able to restore order. But the army had, for years, been complaining about the lack of support and supplies it received from the monarch. The military officers felt that the king had neglected to support them at a critical stage in the war with Israel. Many officers took the defeat personally, and blamed the king for the loss of the war.

One of these officers was Major Gamal Nasser. He and his battalion had been trapped in the Negev Desert by Israeli forces for three months, and had only been released by the armistice agreement. Nasser felt that Egypt could only rise

Major Gamal Abdul Nasser was at the center of the plot to depose King Farouk I of Egypt in 1952, and was later elected prime minister of the new government. Nasser was the first native Egyptian to govern Egypt in almost 2,000 years.

again if it were freed from the constraints and corruption of the monarch—and also from the British troops who occupied their land. Nasser helped form a "Free Officers Movement," and on the night of July 22, 1952, they made their move. The young military men first seized army headquarters, and then took over government offices and broadcasting stations in Cairo.

Farouk understood that, without military support, with rioters running through the streets of Cairo burning houses, he was helpless to rule the land. He abandoned the throne and left Egypt. A new government was formed by the Revolutionary Command Council (RCC), and the young Gamal Nasser soon became its leader.

Nasser's position at the head of the Egyptian government was significant. He had been born in Alexandria, the grandson of a farmer from Upper Egypt. The revolution that Nasser had helped create was also a revolution in leadership, with Nasser the first native Egyptian to govern the land for nearly 2,000 years. The revolution continued with land redistribution and other movements intended to ensure greater equality for all Egyptians.

Nasser's experience during the war with Israel left him committed not to right wrongs but instead to guarantee that Egypt—and its army—would no longer be viewed as backward and incompetent. For this reason, his priority during the early days of his administration was domestic, rather than foreign, policy. His focus was on Egypt—on its development and progress—rather than on Israel.

In the early days of the new Egyptian regime, neighboring Israel seemed to view it with relative interest, particularly in light of the RCC's stated goals of eliminating corruption and assisting the country in achieving greater economic progress. Egypt was the largest Arab state, and required a strong leadership to take the courageous steps toward peace. The popularly supported Nasser government might, Israeli leaders hoped, be willing to risk the progressive path toward peace as part of its break with the old regime and its steps toward modernity.

David Ben-Gurion seemed to propose that peace was

possible if enough space separated the two countries when he said, "A wide, large desert stretches between the two states, and there is no place for border disputes; there was and is no reason whatsoever for political, economic, or territorial disputes between the two neighbors. On the contrary, the cooperation between Egypt and Israel would help Egypt to overcome its political and social difficulties." But distance would not be enough to guarantee peace, nor would a desert ensure that the interests of each nation could remain independent of each other.

Part of the success of the fragile peace lay in the presence of British troops in the Suez area. Egypt was unwilling to risk battle with Israel as long as the British military still lay at its rear, blocking the path to critical supply lines. But following the signing of the Anglo-Egyptian Treaty of July 1954, British troops began the slow process of withdrawal from the area. As the British troops began to leave the region, Egyptian forces slowly started to crop up in the Sinai. Their presence was not simply to act as peacekeepers. By late 1954, a new breed of intelligence officer was emerging in Egypt. Organized into "self-sacrifice squads," or *fedayeen*, these teams of military intelligence officers crossed over the border with Israel, committing acts of terrorism against Israeli citizens and also gathering intelligence. The talk of peace was heard less often, and the proposals for eventually restoring uprooted Palestinians to their native land were replaced by calls for revenge for the Israeli seizure of Arab lands in 1948.

Nasser's prestige was high in the Arab world. Having negotiated the British pullout, he established new relationships with the Soviet Union and with the West. In 1955, Nasser managed a historic signing of a major arms deal with the Soviet Union (the "Czech deal"), which stipulated that Soviet weapons be shipped to Egypt in exchange for cotton. This deal would have great international importance. For years, the Arab nations had traded for weapons only with Britain, the United States, and France. Now, the Soviet Union had entered the weapons business. Soon both the Soviet and Western countries were competing for dominance in the Middle East, and the Israel-Arab conflict began to develop into a truly global conflict.

Up until the time of the Czech deal, Israel had felt confident that its military was the equal of any Arab nation. But the news that superior bombers, tanks, submarines, and anti-aircraft guns were heading into Egypt was a shock to Israeli leadership. It was clear that Egypt would have the ability to launch a war, and that Nasser would soon feel ready to win it.

Israel decided to strike first, before the Soviet arms shipment had been completed and Egyptian soldiers trained in the use of these new weapons. But Israeli leaders did not want to launch an all-out assault on Egypt. Mindful of the need for continued Western support, Ben-Gurion understood that a sudden attack on Egypt would mark Israel as an aggressive warrior rather than a defender of its own interests. The plan required subtlety, to lure Egypt into war without launching an overwhelming opening attack.

Ben-Gurion hoped ultimately to remove Nasser from the political scene, and in the shorter term to defeat the Egyptian army before it could receive the full load of Soviet weapons. The plan was to respond to each Egyptian incursion over the Israeli border, something that had been going on for several months, with greater force, gradually escalating the response until war was inevitable.

Israel did not have to wait long for the first opportunity. On October 26, 1955, Egyptian forces crossed over into the demilitarized zone and raided an Israeli outpost. The next night, Israeli forces responded, attacking an Egyptian

David Ben-Gurion, the prime minister of Israel, shown here in 1947, hoped for peace with Egypt under its new government, but Egypt allied itself with the Soviet Union in its preparations for war with Israel. In 1955, the tensions between the two countries began to escalate, and Israel struck the first blow in the Sinai-Suez War.

outpost in the Sinai Desert. Then they waited, hoping for an Egyptian response that would "permit" them to respond with greater force. But none came.

On November 2, the Israeli forces attacked another Egyptian outpost next to a demilitarized zone and waited for the counter-strike. But again, the Egyptians were not lured into war. Instead, as the Israeli forces were attempting to pinch and pull Egyptian forces into conflict, Egypt and

Syria were signing a mutual defense pact, an agreement that placed Syrian forces under Egyptian command, and pledged Egyptian support should Syria go to war.

And so the Israeli army turned its sights toward Syria, looking for a new source to provoke the much hoped for conflict. On December 11, the Israeli army attacked Syrian camps along the northeastern shore of the Sea of Galilee, claiming that Syrian positions were preventing Israeli fishermen from earning their living by blocking the fish from leaving their corner of the Sea.

Nasser showed remarkable wisdom—or remarkable patience—in refusing to be drawn into battle. And criticism against the Israeli efforts to provoke a crisis were heard, both from Western governments and within Ben-Gurion's own cabinet. Ultimately the plan to strike before Egypt became too strong had to be abandoned, and instead Ben-Gurion determined to finalize an arms deal that would bring Israel back to a more even footing in the arms race with its neighbor. Israel went to the United States and to Britain to request weapons, but was turned down. It was in France that Israel's request was granted. The French were angered by how Egypt's pro-Arab movement was sparking trouble in the French-controlled territory of Algeria, and wanted to further cement their position in the region. France delivered enough arms to Israel not simply to bring them to an equal footing with Egypt, but to ensure that they would have a force superior enough to destroy Nasser's army. The arms race in the Middle East was underway, and war would be the inevitable result.

The final blow was struck not by Israel but by the United States. In July 1956, the United States announced to Nasser that it would not be able to fund the Aswan Dam project, a critical element of Nasser's program for agricultural development of the region. Another partner

In April of 1957, the Italian liner *Oceania* is the first liner to sail through the Suez Canal, after Egypt blocked it off in November of 1956. The Suez Canal was a pivotal territory in the war, claimed early on by Egypt, but later captured by French and British forces.

in the funding, Great Britain, also announced its intention to withhold additional support.

Before a crowd of nearly 100,000 people, the dynamic Nasser made clear that he would not take these setbacks lightly. He proclaimed that Egypt would seize and nationalize the Suez Canal. The waterway was critical to Western interests, and its nationalization would limit or eliminate any ability of Western ships to maintain this important access point to the Middle East. A mere month after British troops had completed their pullout from the Canal Zone, Britain began to make plans to go to war with Egypt. France would join, increasing the speed and pace of arms deliveries to Israel to ensure the participation of Egypt's neighbor in the conflict.

The union of these three countries, each intent on pursuing their own interests in the region, would make war an inevitable consequence. The first strike came from Israel. On October 29, 1956, Israel attacked the Egyptian army, invading Sinai. The United Nations' Security Council, on the very next day, proposed a resolution calling on Israel to withdraw from Egypt, but both France and Britain vetoed the resolution and, the following day, began bombing Egyptian airfields. The Sinai-Suez War had begun.

ARAB FORCES UNITE

Israel's explanation for the invasion, as the war began, was that it was attempting to eliminate the *fedayeen* bases that had been attacking not only across the Sinai border, but along the borders of Lebanon and Jordan, as well. While the Egyptian squads that Israeli forces attacked on October 29 were army bases, not fedayeen, the fedayeen forces quickly responded to the Israeli incursions, attacking two days after the invasion at points in the Gaza Strip and Lebanon and then, one day later, from Jordan and Syria. Nasser's strategy was intended to demonstrate that, although Israel had attacked Egypt, all of Egypt's Arab allies would respond with guerilla tactics. These tactics marked a new kind of warfare— one that was intended to cripple an infrastructure rather than an army, and intimidate civilians, as well. The fedayeen targeted railway bridges, water-pumping facilities, and electrical transformers. They blew up water pipes and planted mines along borders. The message was clear: if Israel attacked one Arab nation, others would come to its aid.

By November 5, Israel's army had seized control of the Gaza Strip and several strategic points along the Sinai Peninsula. The Canal Zone, separating the Sinai from the rest of

Egypt, was quickly occupied by French and British troops. With large numbers of foreign troops occupying Egypt, Nasser was forced to accept a humiliating ceasefire.

For Egypt, and for many other Arab nations, the Sinai-Suez War marked a notable and significant change in foreign policy. Where once the goal for Arab nations had been independence first, and then the removal of foreign powers from the Middle East, the goal now shifted to a desire for revenge, to confront and contain Israel.

For Israel, the war marked an opportunity to expand Israeli territory at Egyptian expense, to demonstrate Israeli power, to take down a mighty army, and to further guarantee Israel's right to exist. The frequent border attacks, the closure of the Suez Canal, had been merely the sparks that ignited many different emotions. Sadly, the war's end would not resolve these differences. It would, in a way, merely guarantee that they would continue.

3

The Myth of a Second Chance

In the aftermath of the Sinai-Suez War, Nasser became an even more polarizing figure in the Arab world. His very presence at meetings served as a reminder of the common enemy Arab nations shared: Israel.

The Nasser model led to revolutions and civil wars that overthrew more conservative governments in Lebanon, Iraq, and Yemen, as well as unrest in Jordan and Saudi Arabia. But the influence of Nasser and his Arab League extended in one other direction: to the union of several Palestinian guerrilla organizations into a single force, to be known as the Palestinian Liberation Organization (PLO). The goal was to organize the Palestinians in a more cohesive way that would enable them to become more actively involved in the liberation of their land. Created at a meeting of 13 Arab heads of state in January 1964, the goal was not necessarily to give the Palestinians a more public forum to air their grievances; it was instead designed to provide some measure of control over the existing guerilla groups, to prevent the Arab states from too soon being drawn back into another war with Israel.

Nasser's Arab League led to the formation of several Palestinian guerilla organizations into the Palestinian Liberation Organization, or PLO, in 1964. Yasir Arafat (shown here), the leader of one of the larger guerilla organizations, became the leader of the newly formed PLO in 1968.

Among these guerilla groups was one of particular interest. The first to be created (in the late 1950s) it was known as the Palestine Liberation Movement, or *Fatah*. Its objective was to use force to destroy Israel. Its founder: Yasir Arafat.

A REVOLUTIONARY'S BEGINNING

The man so closely identified with Palestinian liberation was actually born in Cairo, Egypt, on August 24, 1929—or so his birth certificate states. Like much of Yasir Arafat's earliest life, contradictions abound. In other documents and interviews, he has stated that he was born on August 4, not 24, and in Palestine rather than Egypt. The conflicting reports, the uncertain details of his childhood, have all contributed to the mystery with which Arafat has chosen to cloak his earliest years.

Mohammed Abdel-Raouf Arafat al-Qudwa al-Husseini was known from childhood as *Yasir*, meaning "no problem" or "easygoing" in Arabic. But his life was far from easy. His mother died when he was only four years old, and shortly after her death Yasir and his younger brother were sent to Jerusalem to live with their uncle for four years. The uncle's home was near two sites of religious significance: the "Wailing Wall" (a sacred place for Jews) and the Haram al-Sharif (a holy shrine for Muslims). From his earliest age he was witness to the mounting tensions between Jews and Arabs.

When his father remarried, Yasir and his younger brother returned to Cairo, a city now battling unrest and frequent outbreaks of violence as World War II began and as King Farouq began his first year of rule. The presence of Allied troops nearby had a tremendous influence on the young boy, and from an early age friends and relatives remember him organizing neighborhood children into military formations and pretending that he was leading various expeditions at the head of a motley collection of young soldiers.

The strong sentiment promoting Arab independence and calling for the end to the British colonial presence in Egypt appealed to many young men like Yasir. He and his friends, as they grew older, would spend time in political discussions and in student movements formed to protest the British occupation. By the mid-1940s, many of the leading figures in the Palestinian nationalist movement, concerned by signs that Britain planned to turn their homeland over to form a Jewish state, had relocated to Cairo, where talk of Islamic heritage, plans for military action and greater unity for all Arabs surrounded Yasir.

This is the old city in Cairo, Egypt, in 1977. Yasir Arafat was born here in 1929, and many of his political ideologies were formed here from watching the conflict between the Egyptians and the British.

One such movement was the Muslim Brotherhood, the *Ikhwan al-Muslimun.* Founded 20 years earlier by Sheikh Hassan al-Banna, the underground organization, calling for a return to traditional Islamic values in government, had by the late 1940s grown in popularity among students and the general public in Egypt. With British forces still occupying

Egypt, the movement met in secret, drafting young men who were disaffected by the current state of affairs in the region and training them in military and terrorist tactics. By the time Yasir was 17, the Muslim Brotherhood had joined forces with a group known as the Arab Higher Committee, formed by Palestinian nationalists, and a core group of young militants was receiving training in such skills as making and defusing bombs and other commando tactics.

The loss of Palestinian territory was a humiliating blow to all Arabs, and Egypt was a focal point for much of the anger and calls for revenge. As it became clear that Israel would be granted the status of an independent state, the skirmishes amongst Palestinians and Jews over territory escalated, and neighboring Arab states had been drawn into the conflict. There was disagreement about the best policy to pursue to maintain Palestinian territory. The feeling within Yasir's group was that Arab nations could assist in arming the Palestinians, but they should allow the Palestinians to fight the battle themselves, to make it clear that this was not a spot for foreign intervention but rather a desperate attempt by native people to resist the loss of their homes and land. However, on the eve of Israel's declaration of independence and the withdrawal of Britain from the region, the neighboring Arab states did mobilize their forces and did launch an attack, with what would ultimately prove disastrous results.

In the final days of the war, Yasir (who had traveled with friends to Gaza and then to Jerusalem to aid the Palestinian resistance) joined the floods of Palestinian refugees fleeing their land. He considered himself lucky—unlike the majority of those refugees, he had a home to return to, and the possibility of education and work in Cairo.

By 1949, Yasir had begun university studies in civil engineering, but his grades were poor and his efforts focused more on politics than studying. He was feeling so discouraged by the

Egyptian students protest against Israel and America on the gate of Cairo University in October of 2000. Cairo is a hotbed for recruiting young people to fight against Israel, and has been ever since Arab opposition to Israel became widespread in the 1940s.

events unfolding around him that, at one point, he flirted with the idea of moving to the United States. He went so far as to apply for admission to a university in Texas and spent several months planning for a new life in America. But while he awaited the approval of his visa, he gradually became more aware of, and interested in, the political storm sweeping through Egypt. Whispers of revolution against the weak King Farouk were growing louder; protests against the presence of British troops on Egyptian soil were growing more frequent.

Yasir soon was drawn deeper into the conflict. He wanted to join the Palestinian fighters, but his thinness and small size led many to disregard his potential. They would not make this mistake for long.

A BLOW AGAINST COLONIALISM

While making a half-hearted attempt to complete his university studies, Yasir came in contact with a group organizing protests against the British troops stationed in the Canal Zone. These protests would ultimately spell doom for the king and mark a significant switch in the tactics of the Muslim Brotherhood. Given a quiet nod by the king to proceed with the nationalist movement to get rid of the British, the Muslim Brotherhood switched from focusing more on religion to politics —and to achieving their aims by violent means, if necessary. Their goal was an independent state governed by Islamic law.

As the campaign to harass the British into withdrawing completely from the Canal Zone grew in intensity, Yasir would slip away from classes to join the groups attempting hit-and-run raids against British troops, making contacts with some of the Egyptian military officers who would go on to overthrow the king. He organized a military training camp at the university, serving as the instructor to a class of young guerilla fighters.

During this time, Yasir decided to campaign for the presidency of the Palestinian students' union, a position that was not supposed to be political but served as a forum to unify a large group of students who had been driven from their homeland. The election, held in 1952, was fiercely competitive, but Yasir's campaigning tactics proved successful.

The position would provide Yasir with an important forum to meet large numbers of Palestinian students gathering in Cairo. And he delivered on his campaign promises. He negotiated with the Arab League to ensure that the tuition of Palestinian students was paid. He moved with ease through the complicated corridors of the Egyptian bureaucracy. He proved quite skillful at promoting his cause—and himself. And his rise to power came at an important point in Egyptian history, just as King Farouk was overthrown. The government in Cairo was changing. And Yasir made sure to meet the new players in charge of the country. With a group of students, he drafted a letter to the new government, asking them to remember the Palestinian refugees as they created new policies. The students all pricked their fingers and signed the letter in blood.

Yasir remained at the university for two years after his peers had graduated. He continued to organize students in Cairo, and to join in military actions in the Suez. He also managed to squeeze in a few classes. He often visited the Gaza Strip area, where one of his sisters had settled after her marriage. The tiny stretch of land—a mere 30 miles long and four miles wide—was a center of Palestinian nationalism, a region where many refugees had fled after the war. With each visit there, Yasir would return to Cairo more convinced than ever of the rightness of the Palestinian cause.

The Gaza Strip had become a target for Israeli attacks in those fiery months leading up to war. To the Palestinian refugees crammed into that tiny stretch of land, it seemed that the Egyptians were unable to adequately defend them from these aggressive actions. More and more, the conversation focused on the right of Palestinians to defend themselves, rather than to rely on other Arab nations to do the fighting for them.

Meanwhile, Prime Minister Nasser was focusing his efforts on persuading the British to withdraw from the Suez Canal. As part of the negotiations, he promised to bring an end to the raids on British troops occupying Gaza, and ordered all training centers (including Yasir's) to be closed. The reaction was swift—many frustrated young commandos decided that the best plan would be to assassinate Nasser, to eliminate any possibility of secret treaties with the hated British. The plan failed, many members of the Muslim Brotherhood (the chief plotters against Nasser) were seized, and Yasir, because of his association with the Brotherhood, was arrested. He was held in jail for two months before being released, principally because his accusers could never gather any definite proof that he was a member of the Muslim Brotherhood. Many of the known members of the group were hanged.

Yasir emerged from prison to discover that the climate in Egypt was changing. Nasser was now president, control of the Suez Canal was becoming an international issue, and Egypt would soon be turning to the Soviet Union to arm itself in preparation for war. In August of 1956, Yasir and two of his friends traveled to Prague for an international gathering of students. They were traveling as representatives of Palestine, a significant recognition of the territory as separate and independent from any other nations.

When they arrived at the meeting, Yasir surprised his friends by pulling out of his suitcase a *keffiyeh*, a traditional headdress that had been worn by Palestinians fighting against the British and Jewish settlers in the late 1930s. The *keffiyeh* did startle his friends and they laughed when he first put on the white head-covering. But as Yasir moved among the other students at the conference, he and his friends realized how much attention the headcovering attracted. The *keffiyeh* would become an important part of Yasir's wardrobe in future years, a black and white headdress that would ensure that he stood out at nearly every gathering he attended.

MOVING THE REVOLUTION

When the Sinai-Suez War broke out, Yasir was among a group of reservists called up. His training led him to serve as a bomb-disposal expert during the relatively brief fighting, but in the aftermath of the war, he discovered that the atmosphere in Egypt was no longer healthy for the kind of revolutionary

Egyptian prime minister Gamal Abdul Nasser waves to a crowd in Cairo, Egypt, in June of 1956. He had been at the head of a popular revolution to overthrow the king of Egypt, but the Muslim Brotherhood, a guerilla organization in Egypt, later tried to assassinate Nasser. They were unsuccessful, and had to leave Egypt when Nasser cracked down on them.

talk at which he had become expert. Nasser's interests now lay beyond Egyptian borders, in uniting all Arabs together in a new movement that would continue to provide a realistic threat to Israeli or Western aggression. The interests of a single group—the Palestinians—conflicted with Nasser's vision of one Arab nation bound together by common interests and beliefs, rather than divided by territories or borders.

Yasir graduated from Cairo University in 1956, a full seven years after beginning his studies there. He began a half-hearted effort to pursue a career in engineering, but his heart lay in politics. There was some sense of promise as 1957 began with Israeli troops, under pressure from the United States, starting to pull out of the Gaza Strip. But what was not immediately known was that Nasser, to ensure the Israeli evacuation, had made a secret deal, involving two key promises: that for the next 10 years Egypt would not launch an unprovoked attack against Israel, and that Palestinians would not be allowed to launch attacks against Israel from his country.

Nasser's government began to crack down on all kinds of revolutionary activity. The Muslim Brotherhood was observed carefully. Palestinian groups were under surveillance. And Yasir, known to have ties to both, was on marked time.

"I decided that it was time for me to leave Egypt," he would later recall. "Day by day it was becoming more clear that I would not be free to organize if I stayed in Cairo." His first choice of a new base was Saudi Arabia, but the paperwork involved in moving there resulted in several delays. Finally, looking for a place with greater political freedom—and the opportunity to earn more money as an engineer—he settled on Kuwait.

The land of Kuwait offered the promise of lucrative employment to thousands of Palestinians in the late 1950s. Kuwait, still part of the British Empire, was just beginning to recognize the potential for vast riches—oil—lying buried in its soil. The wealthy Bedouin sheiks who inhabited the stretch of land on the Persian Gulf were willing to import Palestinian labor to do most of the work.

Yasir was given a generous salary for his work on public engineering projects, and soon he had formed his own engineering company, adding to his wealth. But Kuwait provided Yasir with more than financial resources—it offered a new environment to organize a revolution. During the day he would work; nights were reserved for political meetings. By October of 1959, a regular group was gathering to plan an organization that would be independent from other Arab groups, that would focus on Palestinian issues, and that would provide a military framework for reclaiming the lost territory.

Seeking a name for this new group, the members settled at last on Palestinian National Liberation Movement, but they were disturbed to realize that when they abbreviated the name to its initials in Arabic, they were left with *HATAF*, the Arabic word for death. So they reversed the letters to *FATAH*, a word that, in the Koran (the holy book for Muslims), is translated roughly as a way to open the gates to great glory.

Fatah called on Palestinians to join in an armed struggle to regain their homeland. Their message became a rallying cry. From a single group in Kuwait, Fatah soon sparked the creation of several groups in the Middle East and even Europe. Each group contained no more than 10 to 15 members, and more often only two or three, and they were so secret that there was only one contact point—the organizer of the group. Members did not know each other, nor did they know others in other groups. Messages were exchanged by hand rather than by the telephone. Members paid dues and with those plus the wealth of Yasir and other organizers, the groups began to purchase weapons on the black market. To preserve ultimate secrecy, group members were given new names to hide their true identities.

The successful Algerian revolution against the French in 1962 encouraged other Arab groups to press for independence, for the overthrow of foreign regimes. Yasir began to focus less and less on his engineering business and to spend more time traveling throughout Egypt, Syria, Algeria, and Jordan to meet with the revolutionary groups springing up. Yasir's plan was clear: to reclaim the territory that belonged to Palestinians, using whatever force was needed.

But the question of who would be the "official" spokesperson for Palestinian rights was now becoming an issue in the Arab world. Nasser, in an effort to keep the promises he had made to restrain Egyptian and Palestinian violence along the Israeli border, had decided that his safest bet lay in developing his own Palestinian organization, a group that would demonstrate his support for Palestinian interests but ensure that they answered only to him. Nasser invited 13 Arab leaders to Cairo, and initiated the launch of a new group, a group with two sides. The political side, designed to present the official position for negotiations and diplomacy, would be known as the Palestine Liberation Organization (PLO). Its military side— not an independent group, but rather groups of forces subject to the Arab governments—would be known as the Palestine Liberation Army.

In 1964, the PLO held its first conference in East Jerusalem, part of the territory governed by Jordan. They drafted a constitution and a charter, calling for an armed struggle and the ultimate destruction of Israel. The PLO became an important, central core for organizing the many Palestinian groups that had sprung up throughout the Middle East. But it was clearly tied to Nasser and Egypt, and dependent on other Arab nations for its military strength.

Yasir was suspicious of the group from the start. He knew that the secret to success, the core belief of Fatah, was that Palestinians deserved the right to have an independent nation, to rule themselves in their own homeland. He decided that the time had come for action. He gave up his job and left Kuwait. From now on he would no longer be an engineer. Being a revolutionary was now his full-time occupation.

Fatah was rapidly losing support and members as the PLO was launched. To many Palestinians, there no longer seemed to be a need for secret meetings and secret organizations; they could meet in open, under Nasser's sponsorship, to discuss the issues that mattered to them. Encouraged by the PLO's success, and sensing that Fatah would not follow the plan, Nasser took steps to wipe out the remaining opposition. Yasir became a wanted man, and orders were given to stamp out all Fatah groups and eliminate their members.

This was a critical point in the relationship between Israel

Yasir Arafat, shown here speaking at a press conference in Syria in 1969, began his political career organizing students in Cairo, Egypt; he then moved to Kuwait, where he organized a group called FATAH to liberate Palestinians. Arafat's career as a revolutionary has been marked with both successes and failures, but he has always demonstrated complete commitment to his cause.

and the rest of the Arab world. Had Israel better understood the climate in Egypt, it is possible that at this moment in time the government would have recognized that Nasser was doing everything within his power to ensure that he did not have to go to war again with Israel, at least not in the immediate future. Nasser had no intention of fighting another war, a war that he was sure to lose.

But Israel had come into existence fighting, and its people and, more importantly, its leaders, had known nothing but hostility from the Arab world. Its leaders were watching, waiting, following the events in Egypt and other countries and looking for omens of when the next violent outburst would come. They did not have to wait long.

4

Water as a Weapon

In the arid deserts of the Middle East, water is one of the most valuable assets a country can possess, the secret to successful agricultural development, a solution to transportation problems, and a critical strategic advantage for military operations. In the early 1960s, Israel had focused more firmly on domestic development, and the government became interested in developing such agricultural industries as olive oil production. Southern Israel became a target for increased development, and a plan was launched to provide irrigation in this part of the state by using water from the Sea of Galilee. In order to accomplish this, part of the Hula swamps in northern Israel needed to be drained.

As work began in northern Israel, neighboring Syria began to protest at the extent of operations going on in the demilitarized zone separating the two nations. Syria claimed that Israel was changing the terrain—a change that would create more favorable military conditions for Israel—and criticized the seizure of Arab-owned land for the project. Israel claimed that

This is the Jordan River, a body of water that separates Jordan from Israel. As fighting in the Middle East progressed, water became one of the key issues of the conflict.

the project was fully in line with the armistice agreement, since all construction was for a civilian, rather than military, project and would result in greater economic benefits to the region.

At nearly the same time, to the east of Israel, Jordan began construction of a large dam on the Yarmuk River.

The Yarmuk flows across Jordan, ultimately emptying into the Jordan River, a body of water separating Jordan from Israel. Israeli protests against the project began almost immediately, arguing that the dam would decrease the amount of water in the Jordan River.

By 1964, the battle for water was being launched on a new front. At a summit of Arab leaders held in Cairo, it was decided that Lebanon and Syria would launch projects that would further deplete the amount of water available to Israel in the Jordan. The countries would divert the water flowing from two rivers—the Hasbani and Baniyas—into the Jordan.

Israel's response was swift and clear—military attacks were launched against the two construction projects, with bombs sending an unmistakable message. All along the border, forces began to gather. Syrian troops in the Golan Heights began shelling groups of Israeli settlers in the north. Israel responded by launching an air attack, shooting down six Syrian fighter planes.

The Arab world looked to Nasser to respond to the crisis, and he did not disappoint. The Egyptian army was given orders to move into the Sinai Peninsula and soon it had assembled along the Israeli border. The United Nations emergency force patrolling the peninsula was evacuated, and the two armies were nearly face-to-face on either side of the border.

Israel determined not to wait for the first strike to come. On June 5, 1967, Israeli forces launched attacks against Syria, Jordan, Egypt and Iraq. Egyptian ground troops in Sinai and Gaza were severely hit, and nearly all of the Arab air force was eliminated by destructive raids on air bases. Within three days, Egyptian forces were in retreat and Israel held the Gaza and Sinai territory leading nearly all the way to the Suez Canal.

An Israeli tank crew undergoes tank training in May of 1967, the period during which tensions in the Middle East built up to the Six Day War in June. The Six Day War ended with Israel as the victor, having captured about four times as much territory as they had in the previous war.

Israel then moved against Jordanian territory. As fighting broke out in Jerusalem, Israeli forces quickly responded and within two days had seized most of the West Bank as well as the eastern portion of Jerusalem that had been in Arab hands.

A cease-fire was called for on June 8, but Syria refused to comply. The Israeli army, within one day, responded by capturing the Golan Heights. Syria quickly announced that it would accept the cease-fire, and the fighting ended.

Within six days, the landscape of the region had changed completely. Israel now held Gaza, the Sinai Peninsula, the Golan Heights, the West Bank, and all of Jerusalem. The brief war had provided Israel with more than four times the land it had first held following the War of Independence. Jordan had lost most of its major towns—a loss that would cripple the region economically and culturally. It had lost the cities of Jerusalem and Bethlehem, vital sources of income because of the many foreign tourists who visited the region. To add to the problem, refugees fled the Israeli-occupied territory and poured into Jordan, which was left to wrestle with the problem of taking in hundreds of thousands of refugees after losing almost one-half of its source of revenue.

Similar problems greeted Egypt, following the loss of the economic potential of Gaza and the Sinai. Syria, though less crippled by the war's aftermath, was still forced to deal with nearly 100,000 refugees from the Golan Heights and the lost possibility of developing the Jordan Valley.

The war had been swift, but it had proved that even a united Arab army was no match for Israel's military might. The Arab nations would wrestle with their losses—economic, military, cultural, and stature—for many years to come.

PILGRIM TO THE HOLY LAND

In the aftermath of the Six Day War, thousands of Jews streamed into Jerusalem. For so long divided and occupied territory, the region known as the Holy Land was now occupied by Israeli troops, and so for many Jews the period after the war became a time for a pilgrimage to sites held holy by their religion. It was as if most of Israel felt a sudden urge to go sightseeing, to visit the places that had not been open to them for the past 20 years. The portion of Jerusalem that contained the Western Wall was crowded with praying visitors, and Bethlehem and Jericho, too, were crowded with cars and buses as seemingly endless streams of people came to marvel at this site of their ancient history. Jubilant crowds tore down the concrete barricades and barbed-wire fences that had separated the two halves of Jerusalem since 1948.

Among them was a 69-year-old grandmother who would play an important role in Israel's history. Her name was Golda Meir.

Golda had been born in 1898 to a poor Jewish family living in Kiev, Russia. Her earliest memory was of fear—fear of the angry crowds that raged through the streets of Russia, carrying knives and sticks and looking for Jews. It was through her adored older sister that she first began to hear whispers of the Zionist movement, and the dream of establishing a Jewish state where all those suffering from prejudice and discrimination would be free to live, to practice their faith openly and to govern themselves.

The family suffered greatly under the rule of the tsar until they were able to emigrate to America. They settled in Milwaukee, where the young Golda excelled, becoming an outstanding student and quickly learning English. Her parents' home became a gathering place for young men who had volunteered for the Jewish Legion and were going to fight with the British army to liberate Palestine from Ottoman control during the early days of World War I. Their stories inspired Golda, who became convinced that Palestine would one day be her home.

This is Milwaukee, Wisconsin, the home of a Jewish immigrant from Russia named Golda Meir for much of her early life. Meir would later play an important role in Israel's history.

In November 1917, the British government officially announced that it was in favor of the creation of a "national home for Jewish people" in Palestine—a decision known as The Balfour Declaration, so named for the British foreign secretary, Arthur James Balfour, who signed it. Many Jews were inspired to take the step toward emigrating to Palestine.

In 1921, Golda was able to make the longed-for voyage to Palestine, accompanied by her new husband, Morris, her sister, niece, and nephew. Already there were rumors of violence between the Arabs and the Jewish settlers, but the young Golda clung to her idealistic vision of what Palestine would hold.

Her first impression of Palestine, arriving in the 12-year-old city of Tel Aviv after a difficult journey by ship and train, was less than overwhelming. She first noticed the scorching heat, deep sand everywhere, and a few modest stucco houses. The sheets in their hotel room were covered with bedbugs, the fruit in the market was covered with flies, and her first days were a confusing blur of heat and very primitive conditions.

Her first apartment, found with great difficulty and at great expense, had no electricity and no bathroom. The toilets, shared with 40 other people, were located in the yard. Golda and her husband soon moved to a *kibbutz,* one of the collective farms that Jews founded in the region. The idea was to create communities where members were assigned jobs and worked for the greater good of the whole; where meals were eaten in a collective dining room, children lived together in dormitories, and chores were rotated among members, so that all took a turn working in the kitchen and serving meals, and major decisions affecting the settlement were made by the entire community. The concept of kibbutz life—a collective of people with shared ideals building a community—contributed to the rapid development of Israel during its early years.

The communal living suited Golda but not her husband, and so by the 1920s she found herself living in Tel Aviv

and working for the women's council of the Federation
of Jewish Labor, an organization that was rapidly becoming an important focal point for finding jobs for the
thousands of immigrants flooding into the region. It was
at the Federation of Jewish Labor that Golda began to
make the connections that would shape the important
political role she would one day play, as she worked in
close quarters with David Ben-Gurion and other future
leaders of Israel.

A COMMUNITY IN CONFLICT

As Hitler came to power in Europe, thousands of
refugees from Nazism made their way to Palestine,
exhausting resources and seeking housing and employment. The conflict between the Jewish settlers and
Arabs who had inhabited the region before the first
settlements were built increased. Riots grew in frequency,
buses were ambushed, settlements shelled, and the two
communities found themselves at odds on a greater and
greater scale.

The Jewish community was desperate for funds and
weapons to use in its defense. It was decided that Golda
would have the job of traveling to the United States to
speak to Jewish groups to obtain money. Golda was chosen
both because she had lived and traveled in the United
States, and because she was one of the more disposable
members of the senior council governing Jewish affairs. If
something would happen to her en route, if she was
unable to return to Palestine, plans for the new state of
Israel would continue. But it proved a fortunate decision
—during the six weeks she traveled through the United
States speaking to Jewish groups, she raised nearly $50
million, an unbelievable sum and one that enabled the

Adolf Hitler speaks in May 1937; he became the dictator of Germany in 1933, and tried to exterminate Jews, gypsies, and homosexuals, as well as others. Jewish refugees fleeing Hitler's tyranny flooded into Palestine in the 1930s and 40s, creating a shortage in jobs and housing that caused a crisis between Palestinians and Jews in Palestine.

secret purchase of huge amounts of weapons in Europe.

So it was that on that fateful day of May 14, 1948, Golda was among the Jewish leaders who gathered in Tel Aviv to sign the Declaration of Independence of the new state of Israel.

A BRILLIANT CAREER

With the state of Israel less than a month old, Golda received the first "official" appointment of what was to become an unexpected career. She was named Israel's ambassador to Russia. It was considered a surprising appointment for a woman in those years, and a diplomatically important one. A short time into her stay in Russia, she was invited by David Ben-Gurion to return to Israel and become a member of the cabinet he was forming, to serve as labor minister.

Golda returned from Moscow to face a daunting task. As labor minister, she was responsible for solving the problems posed by the nearly 200,000 Jewish refugees who had poured into Israel. These immigrants were being housed, for the most part, in "tent cities," consisting of two families (some from different countries and speaking different languages) per tent. Disease was rampant. These immigrants needed housing and jobs, and they needed them quickly.

Under Golda's leadership, new housing units were constructed and, in a more controversial move, some immigrants were housed in the homes left behind by Arab families who had fled after the wars. New road construction projects were launched, in part to provide employment to the refugees. The projects reshaped the landscape, and Golda coupled them with several social programs that marked the new state, programs to provide insurance, maternity leave and other benefits to workers.

Her elevated position among the founders and leaders of Israel's government led to her next appointment— foreign minister. She was, as always, a controversial choice for the sensitive post in the summer of 1956, as the fedayeen operations were raging along the borders and tensions with Nasser's Egypt were high. Golda, for all her accomplishments,

The Great Kremlin Palace in Moscow, Russia was a place that Golda Meir must have visited frequently in her position as Israel's ambassador to Russia, which was given to her when the state of Israel was less than a month old. She was soon called back to Israel to become the Labor Minister of Israel in David Ben-Gurion's Cabinet.

was not known for her moderate comments or diplomatic skills, and the position directing the activities of Israel's ambassadors and diplomats was considered a stretch for someone with her habit of speaking her mind.

For several years, Golda traveled the globe, firming up ties with African nations, meeting with U.S. presidents, and

Levi Eshkol, the prime minister of Israel and a close friend of Golda Meir's, died suddenly in 1969, leaving Meir as the obvious choice to fill the position of interim prime minister. At the age of 70, Meir came out of retirement to lead Israel, and was elected by a solid majority when her interim period ended.

dealing with the challenges of political infighting in Israel and a never-ending series of tensions with Arab nations. By 1965, suffering from migraine headaches and tired from the nearly endless travel, she decided to retire, to become a full-time grandmother.

Golda experienced the Six Day War as a private citizen, huddling in an air-raid shelter as sirens signaled the start of the battle, and celebrating with joy the news of the quick and decisive end to the military campaign. Her retirement, and the time of celebration, would be short-lived.

On February 26, 1969, Levi Eshkol, the prime minister of Israel and Golda's close friend, died suddenly of a heart attack. In post-war Israel, with elections only a few months away, there was great competition among several different factions to assume leadership of the country. The party was desperate for an experienced candidate who would be able to manage the nation both externally and internally until the next round of elections were held. The choice came down to one person: Golda. And so, at the age of 70, the grandmother came out of retirement, this time to lead her nation.

5

Mixing Oil
and War

Golda's earliest months as prime minister involved an important trip to the United States, where during meetings with President Nixon, she cemented a critical strategic alliance between America and Israel. When her few months as interim prime minister ended, she was elected by a solid majority to the position in her own right.

Golda's background in labor issues and interest in the social environment of Israel marked her term as prime minister. She concentrated on attempts to bring greater equality to all Israeli citizens through social measures that focused on ensuring that Israel's overwhelming defense budget did not remove any available funds for the social issues that mattered to her. Surprisingly, she was a tough negotiator when strikes threatened to disrupt critical services, speaking out strongly against union activities that threatened to slow development or jeopardize national security.

In September 1970, a transition happened that would transform Arab-Israeli relations. Gamal Nasser, who had led Egypt for many decades and whose galvanizing presence had united the Arab world, died. The new Egyptian president, Anwar Sadat, was

Israeli prime minister Golda Meir speaks at a news conference in Washington, D.C. in 1973. One of Meir's first steps as prime minister was to cement an alliance between Israel and the United States; she came to speak with President Richard M. Nixon a few months after her election as prime minister.

initially viewed as a pale substitute for Nasser, a weaker politician whose time heading Egypt would be brief. But those who underestimated Sadat were surprised at how quickly and forcefully he assumed command.

His first step: to encourage Egyptians to move beyond the disgrace of previous unsuccessful wars by taking steps to indicate his willingness to seek a diplomatic solution to the conflict. His first offer—to reopen the Suez Canal if Israeli forces would pull back from portions of the Sinai Peninsula —was rejected by the Israelis. Sadat continued his diplomatic approach, restoring a relationship with the United States and declaring a cease-fire. He also began to distance himself from the Soviet Union, and focus more on establishing firmer relationships with other Arab nations like Syria.

Sadat's meetings with other Arab leaders were not mere diplomatic courtesy calls. He was busily making secret plans for a joint military effort against Israel, going so far as to state, in 1971, that the time of decision had come and Israel must withdraw to its pre-1967 territory. When no immediate action was forthcoming, most nations (including Israel) assumed that Sadat was simply making empty threats.

Golda, meanwhile, was wrestling with the sticky question of Jewish settlers moving into Hebron, a town on the West Bank of the Jordan River. Hebron was important to the Jewish faith as it was thought to be the place where the earliest patriarchs of the Bible are buried. After Hebron was seized from Jordan, it became part of the regions of the West Bank where settlement was forbidden. But a group of young Orthodox Jews forced the issue by moving into the town, in essence daring Golda's government and the military to force them back out.

This they were unwilling to do. The settlement of this territory, which had until recently belonged to Jordan, served to inflame Israel's Arab neighbors. It also sparked violence in the Palestinian community. By 1968, the various guerilla groups that made up the Palestinian liberation movement had, with some difficulty, come together under the single umbrella of the PLO. And with the election of Yasir Arafat as the PLO president, the Palestinian groups began to pull more closely together, almost simultaneously distancing themselves from their earlier dependence on other Arab nations.

Under Arafat's leadership, the PLO became an active force on the international scene, winning the U.N.'s recognition in October 1974 of its right to serve as the official representative of the Palestinian people. It was granted observer status within the U.N. and, in a special honor, Arafat was invited to address the general assembly. Despite its membership in the Arab League, the PLO was often viewed with suspicion or outright animosity by other Arab nations, particularly those with sizeable populations of Palestinian refugees. These nations were fearful of being pulled into battle with Israel, not under their own terms, but rather following guerilla raids against Israel from their borders.

Sadat was more willing than other Arab leaders to speak out for the rights of Palestinians, but he had his own strategic reasons for doing so. Under the guise of calling for a greater recognition of Palestinian rights, Sadat frequently criticized— at the U.N. and in other international forums—Israel's unwillingness to withdraw from conquered territories, in particular the Sinai and Golan, withdrawals that would certainly benefit Egypt strategically.

In May of 1973, Golda was informed by her military commanders that Syrian and Egyptian troops were conducting military exercises along the Israeli borders, and that the number of troops engaged was sizeable. Despite this rather alarming increase in the number of soldiers gathering along the border, Israeli intelligence reports indicated that Sadat would not be willing to wage another war, and most military officers felt confident that their forces were so far superior to any others that an attack would be suicide.

They were wrong. On October 6, Israel was attacked from the south by Egypt, and from the north by Syria. The Egyptian troops crossed the Suez Canal with ease; Syria

Here, an Israeli tank passes the remnants of a Syrian tank in the Golan Heights in Israel during the Yom Kippur/Ramadan War of 1973. In this war, Syria and Egypt attacked Israel to get Israeli soldiers to withdraw from the Golan Heights and Sinai. The war began on October 6, corresponding to Yom Kippur in the Jewish tradition, and Ramadan in the Muslim tradition.

quickly occupied the Golan Heights. The Israeli troops were outnumbered at a rate of nearly 12 to 1 at the beginning, until more reserves were called up for battle. The day the war began had religious significance to both side. For Jews, it took place on Yom Kippur, the Jewish Day of Atonement, and so became known as the Yom Kippur War. For Muslims, the battle began during the month of fasting known as Ramadan, and so for Arab nations the conflict was known as the Ramadan War. For both sides, this holy time of fasting became a period of intense fighting instead.

The conflict quickly drew in critical allies to provide much-needed military equipment and supplies. The United States flew in provisions to Israel; the Soviet Union did the same for its allies, Syria and Egypt. The fresh supplies and the arrival of reserve soldiers began to turn the tide of the battle in Israel's favor. It was able, within a week, to push Syrian forces back from the Golan Heights and, on the other front, cross the Suez Canal and force Egyptian forces to retreat toward Cairo.

By October 22, a cease-fire had been approved. Israel had succeeded in pushing back Syrian troops from the Golan Heights and, in fact, occupying some additional Syrian territory, as well as recapturing the Sinai territory. But, in a strange twist, both Israel and Egypt claimed to have won the war—Egypt for its initial success in pushing into the Sinai, and Israel for ultimately winning back its territory. As both sides had suffered significant losses, both in men and equipment, neither side truly emerged as a winner.

The war had officially lasted only 16 days, but it would have repercussions that would significantly affect the politics of the Middle East for generations. For Golda, it would mark the end of her career as prime minister. The war and its aftermath had caused tremendous dissension in the government and even within Golda's own party. There was great disagreement about the events leading up to the war and Israel's failure to anticipate the invasion. The Israeli people were sick of war, sick of the constant threats, sick of burying their sons and daughters. There was great criticism of the government that had placed them in another war.

For Golda, the time had come to step down. Five years after first becoming prime minister, and some 50 years after embarking on a career in public service, she was tired and unable to resolve the difficulties in putting together a new

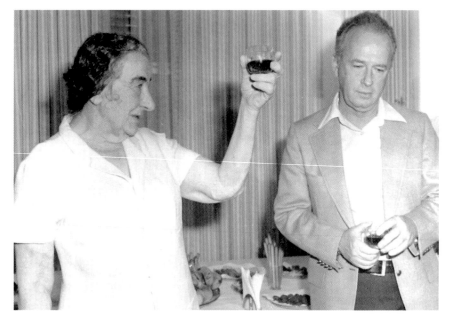

Golda Meir toasts a general of the 1967 war (and later the prime minister of Israel), Yitzhak Rabin, in 1974. Meir was forced to resign her position due to political dissension in the aftermath of the Yom Kippur War.

team that would satisfy all viewpoints. It was time for her to return to private life. The new prime minister would be Yitzhak Rabin, a *sabra*—a native born in the state of Israel, rather than part of the generation of immigrants who first shaped the new nation. It was an important shift in political philosophy, as power gradually was passing into the hands of the children of those early immigrants, children who had been born knowing only Israel as their home.

THE OIL FACTOR

Another result of the Yom Kippur/Ramadan War was the impact it had on the decisions of OPEC, the Organization of Petroleum Exporting Countries. The Arab members of OPEC determined that oil could be used as a way to even the score. The sale of oil—both in terms of quantity available and price—was suddenly linked to the level of support a particular country would offer the Arab nations.

Step one was to cut back on the supply until Israel agreed to acknowledge the rights of Palestinians and give back the territory it had gained in 1967. Needless to say, Israel refused both demands, and the OPEC nations began to cut back on their oil production. The repercussions were almost immediate, as the price of oil streaked up and gas shortages crippled the American economy.

The U.S. secretary of state, Henry Kissinger, launched a series of meetings that would be known as "shuttle diplomacy," traveling back and forth between Israel, Egypt, and Syria to craft agreements that would be acceptable to all sides. Ultimately, he met with some success, and brought about the withdrawal of each side's forces from sensitive regions. But the stepping down in tension would mark a distancing between Egypt and Syria. Sadat was extremely popular following the war, and his post-war compromises were viewed with distaste by the Syrian leader, Assad, who transferred his loyalties to a more militant anti-Israel group that included Iraq, Libya, Yemen, and the PLO.

PALESTINIAN POLITICS

The aftermath of the war also had its effect on the PLO—a change clearly for the better. The PLO began to move away from terrorist activities to focusing more on bringing about change through diplomacy. In June of 1974, the Palestinian National Council met in Cairo and approved a new 10-point plan, which called for revolution in gradual stages, rather than all at once. Within the plan was the clear message that the short-term priority of the PLO would be the creation of a Palestinian state in the West Bank and Gaza Strip. This was a critical change from previous calls for the complete liberation of all Palestinian territory.

The moderate tone and emphasis on diplomacy brought about results. More nations were recognizing the PLO as the legitimate representative of the Palestinian people, and more policymakers were paying attention to the rights of Palestinians to govern themselves. It was becoming clear that the ongoing problem of the Palestinians lay at the very heart of the conflict between Israel and the Arab nations. Until it was resolved, peace in the Middle East might not be easily achieved.

The PLO, by the mid-1970s, had based itself in Lebanon, where Arafat was given the right to control military positions in the south—positions from which an attack on Israel could be launched. In addition, the PLO was allowed to run the refugee camps located in Lebanon, where nearly 300,000 Palestinians were currently living. This opportunity to create a kind of independent government within the borders of another country would divide Lebanon and result in civil war, as the country was torn between those who felt Lebanon should be more closely allied with Arab causes and focus on ensuring more even distribution of resources among all people, and those who favored a more conservative approach to the government and wanted close ties with Europe as well as other Arab nations.

The PLO was quickly pulled into the conflict. As it rallied to one side, Israel began secretly supplying the other. In a way, the Lebanese civil war turned into a kind of Palestinian/Israeli conflict fought on foreign soil. Ultimately, a ceasefire would be declared in late 1976 and Arafat would join with the leaders of Lebanon and Syria to craft an agreement for ending the war.

The war provided Arafat and his Palestinian forces with an opportunity to form critical alliances with Syria, to further establish their position in Lebanon, and to win over more support with their cause by supplying much-needed resources to the Lebanese people. The war had been sparked by the presence of the PLO on Lebanese soil; ironically, it was the PLO that would benefit most from the conflict.

AN IMPORTANT YEAR

The year of 1977 would bring important changes in Israeli-Arab political relationships. In May of that year, a new prime minister, Menachem Begin, was elected in Israel. For the first time since Israel was founded, the Labor party was defeated and a candidate from the Likud party—a party known for its emphasis on increasing Israeli territory—rose to the highest office. One of the most critical campaign issues for the Likud party had been its focus on making sure that the territories in the West Bank and Gaza were retained as part of Israel, while the Labor candidates had hinted that peace could best be achieved if Israel withdrew from the land it had captured in 1967.

Meanwhile, history was changing in another dramatic way. In November of 1977, Egyptian president Sadat made a visit to Israel. It was the first official visit of an Arab leader to Israel since the state had been formed. Sadat spoke before the Knesset, the Israeli parliament, and in that speech outlined his plan for peace and, in a truly dramatic breakthrough, hinted that Egypt would recognize Israel and its right to continue to exist as a Jewish state.

These startling events were, in part, sparked by unrest within Egypt. Sadat, in the early part of the year, had been faced with riots within several cities, protests against increased prices of food and other basic goods. Police stations and the homes of government leaders were targets of much of the rioting, and ultimately the army had to be called in to put a stop to the violence.

Sadat felt that the only way to solve the economic crisis would be to increase the amount of money available for domestic spending, pouring more money into development programs and other plans that would clearly benefit the Egyptian people. This would require reducing the amount of money being spent on the military, on defense and on weapons systems. Sadat also believed that a clear move toward peace would encourage a better relationship with the United States and possibly entice more foreign investment.

Sadat's trip to Israel resulted in a visit to Egypt by Begin on Christmas Day. But it was not a simple matter to change the activities and sentiments of two nations overnight. Despite the historic gestures of exchanging visits, Israel still proceeded with installing new settlements in the controversial region of the Sinai Peninsula. And Sadat was discouraged by the apparent unwillingness of Begin to budge from his firm position that Israel must retain control of the West Bank and Gaza regions. He noted that, without some compromise from the Israeli leader, there was no point to his continued efforts to press for peace.

The American president, Jimmy Carter, sensed that a once-in-a-lifetime opportunity was slipping away, and decided to make a final attempt to bring the two sides together. So it was that in September of 1978 both Begin and Sadat arrived at Camp David in the United States for a truly historic meeting. From September 5 through the 17th, Camp David became the setting for intense debate. President Carter's belief that, by bringing the two men together, a compromise might be easily carved out proved mistaken, as within 10 days the talks had deteriorated to the point that neither Begin nor Sadat would speak to each other. By the 15th, Sadat announced that he was ending the meeting and leaving, but Carter persuaded him to stay with promises for additional support and

Anwar Sadat, the president of Egypt, in a picture taken in 1981, is the successor to Gamal Nasser, the Egyptian president who died in 1970. Sadat, who was initially criticized as a weak successor to the powerful Nasser, became very popular in Egypt following the Ramadan War, for his role in organizing the Arab countries in their stand against Israel.

warnings that an abrupt ending to the meeting would have consequences for the United States/Egyptian relationship.

As the United States held the shaky summit together, it also provided the incentive to come to a reasonable conclusion.

Egyptian president Anwar Sadat (left) and Israeli prime minister Menachem Begin (right) clasp hands with U.S. president Jimmy Carter (center) at the signing of the peace treaty between Egypt and Israel in 1979. Many attempts have been made to establish lasting peace in the Middle East, but there has been no long term success so far.

The United States offer to pay for new Israeli military bases, should Begin agree to give up the airfields in the Sinai and give up the Jewish settlements in the northern part of the peninsula, finally resulted in Israel agreeing to return the region to Egypt. And so the summit came to a historic end, with both sides agreeing to press ahead toward a peace treaty and to move toward full and normal relations.

In the months following the signing of the Camp David

Accord, both Egypt and Israel proceeded as promised. Israel completed the first stage of its withdrawal from the Sinai, and there were exchanges between the two nations of business leaders, professors, and even tourists. By 1980, the diplomatic developments had progressed so satisfactorily that the two countries each established embassies in the other's country.

But the question of the fate of the West Bank and Gaza was never sufficiently clarified by the Camp David accord. The agreement specified a five-year "transition" period, during which the status of the West Bank and Gaza would be determined based on UN security council provisions. While the critical issues affecting the occupied territory were laid out, their resolution or the steps Israel needed to take were not specified in the kind of clear, straightforward language used to resolve the Sinai region.

As a result, Israeli settlements proceeded in the disputed region. It began when the government seized control of vast stretches of land in the region, claiming that they were required for military purposes. But, in fact, the land would ultimately house more settlements, rapidly increasing the number of Israelis living in the occupied territories. Israel also seized control of a large amount of the region's water resources, often diverting water to Jewish settlements at the expense of Palestinian wells.

Much of the push into the West Bank and Gaza was coordinated by Ariel Sharon, who by 1980 was the agriculture minister. Sharon was responsible for overseeing the settlements in the region, and for much of the controversial transfer of land from Arab to Jewish hands for supposed military needs. Sharon would, some 20 years later, become prime minister of Israel, and so it is important to understand his controversial role in the West Bank and Gaza regions to better appreciate his approach to the region as prime minister. Having served as a general in the 1967 war—one of the heroes of that conflict—

he was not inclined to return land that many had given their lives to claim.

The economics of the region became a critical aspect of the ongoing dispute between Israeli and Palestinian leaders. The Israelis argued that increasing the economic relationship between Israel and the West Bank and Gaza would greatly improve the financial picture in the region. They showed that large numbers of Palestinian and Israeli settlers in the occupied territories were traveling to Israel each day to work and then returning to spend their income in the territory. The Palestinians, on the other hand, argued that the fact that so many workers needed to travel to Israel to find jobs demonstrated that Israel was not abiding by the agreement to gradually, step-by-step, ensure the eventual transfer of the region to Palestinian authorities, but were, instead, increasing the dependence of that region on Israel. They pointed out that the housing and education in the territory was far inferior to that within Israeli borders, and that the region was dependent on Israel for nearly all of its trade.

It was becoming clear that the Camp David Accords, while celebrated as a successful movement toward peace by Egyptian and Israeli leaders, brought considerably less joy to the Palestinians. While Egypt and Israel benefited from newly opened borders, from new diplomatic and financial developments, the Palestinian people were left with nothing.

A LAND OF VIOLENCE

By the early 1980s, the Middle East was in turmoil. The Shah of Iran, who had been friendly to Western interests and unwilling to launch any serious attacks against Israel, had been overthrown by a right-wing Islamic group. Under the directives of its leader, Ayatollah Khomeini, the new focus for outrage within Iran became the United States, and shortly after assuming power the group seized American hostages and held them for months. Yasir Arafat supported the new government, and in its earliest stages Iran's new leader made it clear that he supported the Palestinian cause and would assist in the movement to form a Palestinian state.

But Arafat spoiled the relationship by attempting to have it both ways. He courted the new regime in Iran and, once the relationship was formed, attempted to win U.S. support by offering to serve as an intermediary to try to have the American hostages released. While a few African-American and female hostages were released (an event that Arafat would claim to have engineered), the negotiation failed, and Yasir poisoned his relationship both with the United States (for failing to win the

Ayatollah Khomeini, shown here, was the leader of a right-wing Islamic group that overthrew the more neutral Shah of Iran in the early 1980s. Ayatollah Khomeini strongly supported the Palestinian cause, and took American hostages in the 1980s to show his dissatisfaction with America's support of Israel.

release of all hostages) and with Iran (who now viewed him as a tool of American interests). Iran soon invaded another PLO ally, Iraq, and Arafat was caught in the difficult position of trying to choose sides as two of his closest allies fiercely battled each other.

The situation in the West Bank and Gaza Strip offered additional concerns. A clear split was forming in Israeli political thought as the Begin government accelerated the rate of Jewish settlements in the disputed region. Many of the settlers, particularly in the town of Hebron, seemed to be deliberately attempting to provoke the Arab inhabitants, implying that the Arabs were simply temporary inhabitants of a land that God had given to the Jewish people. Civil unrest soon marked the area, and harsh words gave way to harsher actions.

Sharon, now defense minister, made it clear that the violence was the work of Palestinian terrorists. His goal became the elimination of the PLO, and in particular the removal of the threat posed by Yasir Arafat.

The chaos and unrest in the West Bank and Gaza reflected the uncertainty within the Israeli public. Some felt strongly that the violence should not be tolerated; that the region contained Israeli citizens whose rights to live where they chose must be protected, by force if necessary. Others were tired of the years of war, of the constant violence, and feared that a further crackdown in the region would have repercussions throughout all of the state. They felt that steps should be taken to restore the region, gradually, to Palestinians. The economic situation in Israel increased the urgency of the debate. Inflation was high, and many Israelis felt that the money being spent to police and protect the settlers living in the region would be better spent addressing some of Israel's economic woes.

In the election year of 1981, the Likud government was concerned about the rumblings among the public. Step one: address the economic concerns by cutting taxes. Step two: increase the perceived importance of a strong and forceful government by focusing public concern on a nuclear reactor being constructed in Iraq. On June 7, 1981, Israeli jets made the thousand-mile flight to Iraq to bomb the reactor that was being constructed with French technical assistance. Within Israel, the raid was hailed as an immediate success. Internationally, it was viewed with great criticism.

Having won the elections with these quick steps, the government began to accelerate Israeli development of the West Bank and Gaza, believing that the Palestinians could be overcome by sheer numbers. Emphasizing the quick commute between some settlement towns and Tel Aviv, the government began offering subsidized housing at very affordable prices and offering aid not only to homebuyers but to housing developers, as well.

As thousands of Israelis took advantage of the opportunity these new suburban settlements offered, the government took steps to stamp out Palestinian resistance in the region. Newspapers and books proclaiming Palestinian nationalism were banned from the region, and nationalist newspapers publishing in the territory were shut down. In addition, the government took steps to create a Palestinian leadership structure that was separate and apart from the PLO. Teachers at Palestinian universities were required to sign an oath stating that they did not support the PLO, and a new local government was established based on small village leagues, with the leadership of these hand picked from Palestinians who were willing to forego the demands of the PLO to form a government willing to maintain the status quo.

But the artificial nature of these village leagues was very clear, and they were largely ineffective in their attempts to represent Palestinian people. As the year of 1982 began, tensions within the region were extremely high. And the situation outside Israel's borders would pose an even greater threat to peace in the Middle East.

6

A Shattered
Peace

The 1980s began under a cloud of steadily increasing tension in the Middle East. The cloud first settled over Egypt. Anwar Sadat had been a hero in his country, hailed for his initially tough stance against Israel and then, ultimately, his successful peace negotiation at Camp David. But the glow had soon faded from the accords, as it became clear that the promised-for move toward liberating the West Bank and Gaza was not happening. Sadat's willingness to continue to deal with Israel, despite what many viewed as a betrayal of the Camp David accord, suddenly turned the tide of public opinion away from him and he found his government confronting new challenges from an angry populace.

Egypt was struggling with some of the same economic problems that were confronting Israel. Inflation was high, and while some wealthier Egyptians seemed to be benefiting from an increase in foreign investment, the average Egyptian saw little improvement in his or her way of life. The gap between richer and poorer was growing, and the government was perceived as

Egyptian president Anwar Sadat shakes hands with American president Jimmy Carter in the Oval Office of the White House in 1979, right before Sadat signs the peace accords with the Israeli prime minister. Sadat was assassinated in 1981, only two years after this picture was taken, and his successor, Hosni Mubarak, took steps to ensure that the peace accords were followed.

corrupt and insensitive to the needs of the general public.

As Sadat became aware of the growing chorus of opposition rising around him, he took steps to quiet it by arresting political figures who had been speaking out against his government, many of them representatives of Islamic militant groups. As had so often occurred in the past, the combination of an oppressive government and forceful censorship of opposing views led to an explosion.

On October 6, 1981, a military parade was organized to celebrate the anniversary of the War of 1973. Sadat was seated prominently on the reviewing stand to salute the various units of the army as they passed by. But one unit contained four Muslim fundamentalists who were outraged at the recent decisions of their president. As these four soldiers marched past the reviewing stand, they stopped and fired directly at the president, killing him.

Sadat's vice-president, Hosni Mubarak, became president and quickly took steps to quell the unrest that had culminated in Sadat's assassination. First, he released some of the political opponents who had been jailed, then took steps to ensure that trials were held for members of the government who had been accused of corruption. At the same time, he publicly declared his support for the Camp David Accords, and his wish to continue the path towards peace begun by Sadat.

Israel did not make this path any easier. On December 1981, Israeli armed forces seized the Golan Heights, a strategically important territory that contained thousands of Jewish settlers but was scheduled to be returned to Syria. The inhabitants of the region immediately responded by going on strike, refusing to pay taxes to Israel, refusing to work, and shutting down schools and businesses.

With this somewhat foreboding event, Israel still followed through on its agreed-upon withdrawal from the Sinai Peninsula in April 1982, and the land was returned to Egypt. These events inspired increased violence in the Gaza Strip and West Bank, as settlers and Palestinians clashed more and more frequently.

As spring turned into summer in that year of 1982, Israel soon began looking for a more effective way to stamp out Palestinian violence, by tracing it back to its PLO roots— the PLO military and political headquarters in Lebanon. On

June 6, Israel began what it called "Peace for Galilee," a military campaign designed to completely erase the PLO.

WAR IN LEBANON

The Israeli army pushed forward rapidly, moving across their northern border and then on and up into Lebanon until they were shortly within sight of Beirut. The news came to Yasir Arafat as he was meeting with Arab leaders in Saudi Arabia. He decided to race back to Lebanon, traveling first by private jet (courtesy of his Saudi hosts) to Damascus and then speeding from Damascus to Beirut in his bullet-proof limousine before the roads into the city were cut off by Israeli troops.

Finally reaching the PLO base, Arafat began to plot his strategy. The PLO was caught in a serious trap. In Lebanon, they had attempted to convert a crack force of guerilla fighters into a conventional army. They could not be a match for the overwhelming Israeli military forces, and were engaged in the kind of combat that ill-suited their skills and tactics.

Defense Minister Ariel Sharon, enjoying overwhelming success in the first phase of the campaign, extended the operations. Moving beyond his stated goal of eliminating the PLO presence in southern Lebanon, his troops soon were pushing further northward, bombarding Beirut and producing the kind of cataclysmic destruction that killed thousands of civilians and left tens of thousands more homeless refugees.

Sharon soon had made contact with the Christian-led opposition forces in Lebanon. Sharon's plan was to unite the opposition forces and the Israeli army, to set up a new government in Lebanon that would be friendly to Israeli interests and, as an added bonus, to use Lebanese territory as a launching pad for an assault against Syria.

In the summer of 1982, the Israeli army began a military campaign with the stated aims of erasing the PLO to ensure peace in Galilee, but the campaign extended into neighboring Arab countries. The army pushed on to the town of Beirut in Lebanon, and bombed it. Here, Yasir Arafat inspects the damage done in Beirut in August of 1982.

Outraged Israeli citizens soon understood that their army, rather than engaging in a brief effort to stamp out PLO-sponsored violence within their borders, was instead engaged in a brand-new war against their Arab neighbors. It was a turning point in the history of Arab-Israeli conflict, as large numbers of Israeli citizens began speaking out publicly against the war.

Within one week, Israeli forces had done serious damage to nearly one-quarter of the Syrian air force and were occupying a significant stretch of Lebanese territory. On June 11,

Israel declared a cease-fire but with one important provision—the cease-fire did not apply to PLO forces.

For the next several weeks, Israeli forces continued to bombard Beirut in the hopes of pressuring the Lebanese to force Arafat and the rest of the PLO leadership out of hiding and, ultimately, out of Lebanon. The Lebanese were in no position to defend the PLO. But Arafat did not want to be seen caving in to Israeli demands, nor did he want his forces to submit to the humiliation of a hasty retreat. Arafat agreed in principle to leave Lebanon, but on his terms.

As Israeli bombing of Beirut continued, the pressure of world opinion began to fall more heavily on Israel. The sight of a nation's capital city reeling under the destruction of a vastly superior army made for powerful images, particularly since so many civilians were dying in the process. The quick and easy entry of the Israeli army into Lebanon, the first waves of success and promise of the rapid turnover of governments to a more Israeli-friendly regime, were disappearing as week after brutal week passed without an agreement and with the army fighting a public relations disaster as well as attempting to extract Arafat and the PLO from their strongholds in Beirut.

By early August, Defense Secretary Sharon, now facing opposition from fellow cabinet members, determined that the best way to end the war was to personally target Arafat. This personal targeting forced Arafat to move from one bunker to another, changing locations every two days. Israeli jets were constantly bombarding his location, seemingly able to find his new headquarters after every move.

For both sides, the goal of the war had changed. For the PLO, the war would be a success if they managed to keep Arafat, their figurehead and symbol to the world of their revolution, alive. For the Israelis, the war would end when Arafat was dead.

It took the intervention of another leader to bring an end to this bloody chase. U.S. president Ronald Reagan, outraged by the seemingly senseless Israeli actions—the killing of thousands of innocent civilians and the destruction of a city and most of a nation in their pursuit of one man—finally called on Prime Minister Begin to bring an end to the war immediately. If he refused, Reagan warned, the United States would stop its efforts to negotiate the PLO's withdrawal from Lebanon.

During this heated conversation, President Reagan grimly commented that what Israeli troops were doing was a holocaust. After a long pause, Begin, who had been born in Poland, replied, "Mr. President, I'm aware of what a holocaust is." A short time later, the bombing of Beirut ended.

PLO forces were allowed to withdraw from the territory under the protection of an international contingent of U.S., French, and Italian troops. The PLO traveled first to Cyprus, where they would then fan out to the various Arab nations that had agreed to host them. The PLO headquarters would soon be established in Tunisia.

As Israeli troops began their planned withdrawal, electricity was restored to Beirut, and a new Lebanese president, Bashir Gemayel, was elected. It seemed like a brand-new era in Lebanon, one for which the Israelis felt some measure of satisfaction, but it would be short-lived. The international peacekeeping forces withdrew, and a few days later tragedy struck. The newly elected Lebanese president was assassinated at his headquarters by a bomb blast, later attributed to the Syrian National Party. In response, Lebanese Christian militia, allied with Israel, entered two Palestinian refugee camps and murdered hundreds of men, women and children in an attempt to seek out any remaining PLO members who might have contributed to the assassination.

The international community was outraged at the brutal

American president Ronald Reagan speaks before a joint session of Congress in 1982 to give his State of the Union address. It was only with his intervention on behalf of the PLO that the Israeli army ceased their campaign to assassinate Yasir Arafat.

accounts of the murders. Israel was charged with being in violation of international law. More importantly, as word of the massacre reached the Israeli public, their outrage was as great as that of the world community. On September 29, an estimated 400,000 Israelis—nearly 10 percent of the country's population—gathered in Tel Aviv in a huge rally to demand punishment for those responsible for the massacres. Reluctantly, Begin agreed and a commission was appointed to investigate what had happened.

While clearly the highest levels of Israeli government had been aware of the action, the brunt of the criticism was reserved for Defense Minister Sharon. He was charged with being personally responsible for failing to prevent or reduce the chances of the massacre, and the commission made it clear that he should either resign or be removed from office by the prime minister. Sharon ultimately resigned, although he remained in Begin's cabinet.

The war would cause tremendous damage both within and outside Israel. Thousands of civilians were murdered, much of Beirut was destroyed, the government of Lebanon suffered tremendous upheaval, and hundreds of Palestinians were massacred. Begin would also decide to resign within the year. The PLO, the target of the invasion, would relocate but continue to grow in influence, particularly among the residents of the West Bank and Gaza.

And what of Ariel Sharon, the architect of the invasion and the one found principally responsible for its brutal conclusion? A brief 19 years later, the memory of the disgraceful circumstances of the War with Lebanon would have faded, and Sharon would become Israel's prime minister.

INTIFADA BEGINS

Over the next few years, the climate in the contested West Bank and Gaza regions became explosive. The military occupation of the region did not end in the aftermath of the War with Lebanon, and the army's failure to rout the Palestinian presence in Lebanon and the ensuing disgraceful end to the war made, some felt, the armed presence even harsher in the occupied territories. Nearly half of the land in the West Bank and nearly a third of that in Gaza was gradually being taken over by Jewish settlement and other Israeli use. Palestinian farmers, whose land was being seized, found it increasingly difficult to earn a living in their own territory, and many were forced to commute to Israel, or leave their home for other Arab countries, to take on minimum-wage jobs. The Israelis were in charge of the distribution of water and electricity, and their control of these important resources left many Palestinians lacking both.

By 1987, a new climate was clear in the occupied territories, fueled in large part by the growing number of rebellious Palestinian youths. They had grown up under Israeli occupation, seen the oppression of their parents, and understood that the stance their parents had taken had, for the most part, failed to effect any kind of significant change. They were becoming more politically active, and they had no intention of accepting the status quo.

On December 8, the status quo ended for good. A road accident caused by an Israeli army transport killed four Palestinians who were returning from work in Israel. Their funerals became the focus for mass demonstrations against Israeli occupation. The demonstrations turned into riots. The region had entered a brand-new age, once known as the *Intifada*, a word literally translated as "shaking off" but more accurately defined as resistance.

As the rebellion spread, the Israeli government announced that the disturbances would be stopped with a policy of "might, power and beatings." Thousands more Israeli troops were brought in to police the territory, and arrests and curfews were frequent. But the resistance continued. Young people, even children, were seen throwing rocks at Israeli soldiers. Palestinians refused to work in Israel. The "Green Line"—the border that had once marked where Israeli territory (before 1967) ended and where the occupied territories began—a line that some thought had disappeared—was restored.

The rebellion had come shortly after a peace initiative had

In December of 1987, a road accident caused by an Israeli army truck killed four Palestinians returning home from work. This event sparked large-scale *Intifada*, or resistance, in the Palestinian population in the West Bank and Gaza Strip regions. Here, Palestinian fighters resist Israeli soldiers in the streets.

been launched by King Hussein of Jordan. Hussein had gathered a group of Arab leaders in Jordan in November of 1987 to discuss such issues as restoring relations with Egypt (which had ended when Anwar Sadat signed the Camp David Accords) and the proper position to take in the Iran/Iraq War (the nations agreed to support Iraq). The status of the Palestinians was lower on the agenda.

This was viewed as a clear sign to the Palestinians that their future depended on them. Their Arab neighbors would focus on their own interests first. The PLO was in exile in

Tunisia and unable to participate in the day-to-day struggle.

And so the resistance began at the local level, and benefited from assistance from various Islamic groups, such as the Muslim Brotherhood and a new organization that had appeared sometime in 1985 or 1986, known as the Islamic Jihad. The Muslim Brotherhood's focus had been on religious, rather than political, goals. The Islamic Jihad was a brand-new entity, an organization that survived in small, independent cells consisting of four or five men. They were instrumental in the riots in December 1987, and they often organized under the cloak of mosques, using the loudspeakers that called Muslims to prayer to instead broadcast instructions to those plotting resistance.

Soon, a split began to develop between the Islamic Jihad and the PLO. The PLO's calls for a two-state solution to the crisis, with territory divided between Israel and Palestine, did not satisfy the Jihad. They called for the complete liberation of all Palestine, in essence demanding the elimination of the state of Israel and labeling all Jewish people as their enemies.

By 1988, Israeli forces had cracked down on the Islamic Jihad movement and arrested many of its leaders. To fill the void, a third Islamic group rose to the forefront. This new group was called *Harakat al-Muqawama al-Islamiyya*, the Islamic Resistance Movement, although it quickly became known by its acronym, *Hamas*. *Hamas* is an Arabic word that can be translated as "zeal," and its members brought a much more militant approach to the resistance. Officially a branch of the Muslim Brotherhood, Hamas soon announced that its goals were not the quiet resistance and religious priorities that had marked the Brotherhood. It was advocating a militant approach to the struggle, with little room for compromise, and its new recruits would be the young and the well educated.

The charter that Hamas adopted in August 1988 showed that the philosophy central to the group's core beliefs was markedly different from that of the PLO. The group advocated the presence of Islam as the core of their movement, and noted that there should be no compromise with Jews. The group also focused on social as well as political causes, advocating a more even distribution of resources and a focus on the needs of the poor.

The activities of Hamas and the Palestinian resistance sent a message to leaders of neighboring Arab nations. It was a reminder that Palestinians were not the only Arabs unhappy with the status quo—there might be other rebellions in other places. Corrupt and authoritarian governments were put on warning—they would ignore the crisis in Palestine at their own peril.

THE RESPONSE TO RESISTANCE

One of the earliest to respond to the intifada was King Hussein of Jordan. In July of 1988, he announced that he was giving up all claims to the West Bank. The territory had been seized by the king's grandfather in 1950, and despite the Israeli occupation, the Palestinians in the territory had been officially considered citizens of Jordan, even using Jordanian money and voting in Jordanian elections.

King Hussein had chosen to give up the territory not simply because he believed in the cause of the intifada. He was under pressure from the United States to intervene in a new peace process the Reagan administration was launching—a peace process that would exclude the PLO and instead replace Jordan as the key negotiator on behalf of the Palestinian cause. King Hussein had no wish to interfere in that particular nightmare, and he was also concerned by the rumblings he was hearing from those Jordanians who had been born in Palestine. There was an increasing number of demonstrations on Jordanian soil on behalf of the intifada—Hussein had no wish to see the resistance movement spread further.

Hussein's announcement, greeted with celebration amongst the Palestinians, had consequences for the PLO. The Palestinian residents of the West Bank were no longer Jordanian citizens. Jordanian teachers and government officials who had lived in the West Bank were fired. Palestinians were no longer eligible to hold Jordanian passports. It was now up to the PLO to pick up the pieces— to follow through on their speeches proclaiming the rights of the Palestinian people by providing some concrete actions to make these rights a reality.

For Arafat and his team, it was time to press forward. They knew that the Israeli government understood that the intifada had put in motion a chain of events that could spell disaster for the region. Suddenly, the PLO was beginning to seem like a more moderate voice for the Palestinian cause, willing to accept a compromise solution of two states rather than the complete annihilation of Israel.

In November of 1988, the "Intifada Meeting" was held in Algiers, at which time the Palestinian leadership announced the formation of a Palestinian state, whose capital would be Jerusalem, and a peaceful solution to the conflict. In April of 1989, Arafat was elected as the first president of the state of Palestine.

PEACE IN A TIME OF WAR

In May of 1989, the Israeli government announced that elections would be held in the West Bank and Gaza to select representatives to negotiate peace with Israel. The Israeli plan recognized the need for greater Palestinian independence in the occupied region. It emphasized the importance of the cooperation of other Arab states in the ongoing peace process. It also proposed an interim period, during which elections would be held for Arab residents of the occupied regions to set up a self-governing administration as a way of "testing" the possibility of coexistence before moving further toward a final settlement.

The proposal raised many questions about how the elections would be held, whether PLO members would be eligible to serve as representatives, and whether the ultimate goal would be Israel's full withdrawal from the region. The answers were not clear, and discussions amongst Egyptian, Israeli, and American representatives only served to further muddy the debate.

And then, on August 2, 1990, Iraq invaded Kuwait. The Gulf War divided the Arab world into supporters of Saddam Hussein, the president of Iraq, and those who felt he had unjustly invaded another Arab nation. When the United States responded by organizing a coalition to send in troops to halt the invasion, the war became a kind of referendum against the United States, as much as against Iraq. On the side of Saddam Hussein were Libya, Sudan, Yemen, and Jordan. Also speaking out in support of the Iraqi leader was Yasir Arafat.

It would prove a costly mistake. Arafat would lose the financial and diplomatic support of Saudi Arabia and Kuwait, both of whom had provided vast sums to assist the Palestinian cause. It would alienate Yasir from other Arab countries as well, countries that had supported his campaign for Palestinian rights but could not understand his willingness to support the invasion of another Arab nation. It also gave Israel an opportunity to crack down even further on the West Bank and Gaza, imposing strict curfews when Tel Aviv and Haifa in Israel became the target for Iraqi missiles.

In August of 1990, Iraq invaded Kuwait, a move that sharply divided the Arab nations of the Middle East. The United States quickly responded, sending troops to the region to fight against the Iraqi army, signaling the beginning of the Gulf War. Here, troops of the U.S. 1st Cavalry Division deploy across the Saudi desert in November of 1990.

After Iraq's defeat at the hands of the U.S.-led alliance, peace in the Gulf region became an international priority, and focus turned to the Arab/Israeli conflict as an important piece in the Middle East puzzle. Peace initiatives begun in October 1991 finally began to bear fruit in January 1993 when the Knesset, the Israeli parliament, announced that it was repealing its 1986 law making contacts with the PLO illegal. It was gradually becoming possible for Israel and the PLO to take steps toward peace.

OSLO ACCORD

The Knesset's statement was a reflection of what was going on behind the scenes in Oslo, Norway, where representatives from the PLO and Israel were engaged in meetings, hosted by the Norwegian foreign minister, focusing first on economic issues and then, gradually, moving toward discussions about other areas of possible cooperation. The meetings were held in utmost secret, but those studying the political scene in Israel suspected that the climate might be ripe for change.

A new government had been elected in June of 1992—a government headed by Prime Minister Yitzhak Rabin. Rabin had been a general in the 1967 war—the general, in fact, who had helped capture the West Bank and Gaza territories. No one could accuse him of simply "handing away" the territory—since he himself had fought fiercely to capture the land, he could craft a reasonable plan that would lead Israel slowly and carefully down the path toward peace. As a first step, Rabin announced that many of the settlements that had been established in the occupied territories were based more on political rather than security needs, and he eliminated their funding as well as the construction of new settlements.

The PLO was now faced with a new challenge. Hamas was increasing its terrorist activities in the region, believing that progress could only be achieved through violent acts. Israel responded by deporting many of the Islamic fundamentalists behind the attacks, and so Hamas called on the PLO to stop the talks and cease negotiations with Israel. Meanwhile, much of the PLO's funding from places like

Yasir Arafat gestures while speaking to loyalists of his Fatah group in Ramallah in 1999. Arafat is a controversial figure, the leader of the PLO and a representative answerable to the Palestinian people. In 1992, he and the then-prime minister of Israel, Yitzhak Rabin, met to try to reach a peaceable agreement for the future of Israelis and Palestinians.

Saudi Arabia had been cut off following the Gulf War.

The PLO was at a crossroads. Should they step away from their radical, revolutionary past? Should they cut ties with an important faction of Palestinians and take a chance on negotiations with Israel? Could they really take on the challenge of shaping history and beginning the process of trying to create a new state out of the chaos that reigned in the occupied territories? And, perhaps most important, could they trust Israel to hold up its end of whatever compromise was worked out?

The challenge lay principally with Yasir Arafat. As the earliest symbol of the Palestinian liberation movement, as the figure who represented, more than any other, the face of the Palestinian people, it would fall to him to unite all Palestinians—the radical as well as the conservative—to accept whatever compromise could be worked out. In a sense, he would need to announce that the revolution had ended and present to his people an acceptable future based on an agreement with their historical enemy.

For both Rabin and Arafat, the stakes were quite high. Both were risking their careers—and in some ways, their lives—on a successful outcome. A draft agreement was finalized in Norway on August 19, with high-ranking officials from both sides in attendance. The agreement, known as the "Declaration of Principles on Interim Self-Government Arrangements," required the PLO to recognize Israel's right to exist and to cease terrorist activities. The agreement in turn required Israel to recognize the PLO as the official representative of the Palestine people and to begin the process of a rapid withdrawal of Israeli armed forces from the occupied territories. The agreement spelled out the steps by which the region would move toward independence, first through the election of a Palestinian council which would ultimately become responsible for governing Gaza and the West Bank. Israel retained the right to maintain overall security in the region and to oversee the Jewish settlements. The agreement specified a two-year period before the next stage of negotiations would begin, over remaining issues such as East Jerusalem, the Jewish settlements, and Palestinian refugees, and a five-year deadline for putting into place a final solution for the territory.

Both sides ratified the agreement following a vote from the Israeli cabinet and the Fatah central committee. Rabin commented, following the successful vote, "Every change has its risks, but the time has come to take a chance for peace."

Both leaders would take one more chance for peace, during a historic meeting on September 13, 1993, with U.S. president Bill Clinton. On the White House lawn, following a meeting in which the agreement was symbolically signed in the presence of numerous witnesses, Rabin and Arafat shook hands. It was an amazing sight—the official representatives of two peoples that had spent the better part of a century battling over a narrow strip of land now joining hands and signaling their willingness to lay down their weapons.

7

The Price of Peace

The historic handshake between Yasir Arafat and Yitzhak Rabin seemed a thrilling end to decades of conflict. But in a way, it was merely a stop along the path both the Israelis and Palestinians seemed fated to walk. While large groups of people celebrated the outcome and looked forward to the future, there were others outraged by the compromises their leaders had been willing to make.

For Arafat, the price would be paid in Arab support. Many of the Arab leaders who had previously been his allies—people like Saddam Hussein—were furious at the sight of him side by side not only with an Israeli leader, but an American as well. For them, the linkage with American interests was every bit as much a betrayal as the compromises with Israel.

For Rabin, the price would be even steeper. On November 4, 1995, a rally was held in Tel Aviv to celebrate the ongoing peace process. Tens of thousands of people gathered to sing and cheer. As the rally ended, Rabin spoke quietly to his foreign minister, Shimon Peres, noting that he had received reports that Hamas

American president Bill Clinton (center) presides over peace talks between the Israeli prime minister Yitzhak Rabin (left) and the PLO leader Yasir Arafat (right) in 1993. This was an important moment in the history of the Middle East, as a Palestinian leader and an Israeli leader could shake hands and meet on peaceable terms.

was threatening a terrorist attack on the rally and that the two of them, as a safety measure, should leave separately. Peres walked down the stairs first, and as he was getting in his car, he heard three shots fired behind him. Prime Minister Yitzhak Rabin was dead, killed not by a Palestinian terrorist but instead by Yigal Amir, a right-wing Jewish fundamentalist.

Shimon Peres became the new prime minister, vowing to follow through on all of the commitments his predecessor had made. And so once more officials from Syria and Israel gathered in the United States on December 27, 1995, at a remote location in Maryland near the Wye River. The first part of the meetings focused on "normalization" issues—things like opening embassies in both countries, canceling Arab boycotts on Israeli goods, and interconnecting roads and telecommunication. Phase two, in late January, focused on security issues, principally on the status of the Golan Heights.

It was at this stage that the talks broke down. Prime Minister Peres felt things were progressing too slowly. He wanted to hold new elections, to make sure that he had the support of the Israeli people before proceeding further. But the meeting truly came to an end when a renewed outburst of violence in Jerusalem by Hamas left many Israelis dead or wounded. The peace negotiations were over.

PEACE WITH SECURITY

Peres had decided to hold general elections as a way to confirm public support for the actions of the Labor Party, as an affirmation of the progress achieved by both his own and Rabin's administration. The results would prove disappointing. On May 29, 1996, Peres was defeated in his bid for re-election and a new prime minister, Benjamin Netanyahu, was appointed as the representative of the Likud Party.

It was as if the Israeli voters had chosen to step back in time. Netanyahu, a youthful and cosmopolitan prime minister, still surrounded himself with the faces of the Likud past, including Ariel Sharon. Netanyahu's campaign slogan had been "peace with security," and this became the theme of his administration. Most Israelis were outraged by the Hamas terrorist campaign just as peace was seeming to be possible, and this outrage and disgust contributed in no small part to the votes for what was perceived as a more "hard-line" candidate.

Israeli prime minister Benjamin Netanyahu addresses the Council of Jewish Federations in Annapolis, Maryland, in 1997. Netanyahu was elected prime minister after Shimon Peres, the interim prime minister (after the assassination of Yitzhak Rabin in 1995), held a general election. Netanyahu did not hold with the 1993 peace agreement between Israel and the PLO, and a new agreement was reached in October of 1998.

Netanyahu was no fan of Arafat, and he felt that the previous administration had been too willing to compromise to achieve peace. Within three months, he was making clear his reluctance to accept many of the terms of the Oslo Accord and the agreement with the Syrians. He began to expand the settlements in the disputed territory, and indicated that he was not willing to withdraw Israeli troops from the Golan, part of the initial informal understanding achieved with Syria.

The status of the players had changed when once more they gathered in October 1998 at the Wye River site in Maryland. President Clinton was battling a series of personal and political scandals that threatened to wreck his presidency. Israel was now represented by Netanyahu, who made it clear that he would not be restricted by earlier agreements nor the more compromising attitude of previous Israeli administrations. Yasir Arafat had received tremendous criticism, both from Palestinian hardliners and other Arab leaders, for his willingness to make a deal with the Israelis, and now he was unwilling to appear weak or eager for an agreement. The group was joined by King Hussein of Jordan (Hussein had left a hospital where he was being treated for the cancer that would soon kill him), who hoped to add his own personal influence to the meeting.

After nine days of difficult negotiations, an agreement was finally reached to begin the process of resolving the status of the disputed territory. King Hussein would quote Yitzhak Rabin when, at the conclusion of the meeting, he would say, "Enough destruction, enough death, enough waste." But this hopeful statement would prove false.

A COMMON HOMELAND

The politics of Israel have been deeply scarred by the conflict with Palestinians and with neighboring Arab nations. The rise and fall of administrations in the last few decades has reflected, in many ways, popular support for a particular strategy for achieving peace. The compromises made by Yitzhak Rabin—to hand over portions of the West Bank to Palestinian control—led to violent reprisals and Rabin's own death. The violence brought forward a new prime minister, Netanyahu, whose more confrontational approach to the peace process appealed to frustrated Israeli citizens.

Under Netanyahu, a new agreement was reached that

called for the handing over of additional territory—this in the city of Hebron—to Palestinian control in 1997. But even Netanyahu was unable to hold onto power long enough to oversee the next step in the peace process—further withdrawals from the occupied territories.

His successor was Ehud Barak, who had been involved in earlier peace negotiations with Syria as part of the Peres government, and who promised to focus on bringing an end to the Israeli-Arab conflict. His plan was to continue peace talks with the Palestinians, re-start peace talks with Syria, and withdraw Israeli troops from southern Lebanon.

It was an ambitious program—and perhaps an impossible one—requiring diplomatic focus on three sensitive areas. Was it reasonable to expect Israel to withdraw from the Golan Heights (turning the land back to Syria) and southern Lebanon, as well as to hand over control of the West Bank and Gaza to Palestinians, all in a year, as Barak had promised when elected in May 1999? Perhaps not. He would ultimately prove unable to build a lasting peace with the Palestinians, and a difficult round of meetings hosted by President Clinton in 2000 at the presidential retreat, Camp David, would end in Barak and Arafat unable to reach agreement.

Elected on a promise of peace, Barak would be defeated when he failed to achieve it. The public perception, perhaps unfair, that he would be willing to trade away Jerusalem for peace led to the defeat of his government in elections held in 2001. And, as hopes for peace were dashed, violence in the West Bank and Gaza increased.

SECOND INTIFADA

The second intifada—the second intense round of Palestinian resistance—began in response to the failed peace process. In December of 2000, Palestinians took to the streets to mark the

Current Israeli prime minister Ariel Sharon, who was elected in 2001, is best known for his involvement in a massacre in a Palestinian refugee camp in 1982. One of his campaign promises was to deliver not peace, but security to Israel. He is another extremely controversial figure in the struggles between Israel and the Palestinians.

anniversary of the first intifada and to demonstrate their frustration at the lack of a resolution to their status.

What was intended as two days of protests evolved into an ongoing cycle of violence. Unlike the first intifada, where many of the protests were non-violent, the newest round of resistance was marked by death and destruction, and the loss of hundreds of lives, the majority of them Palestinian. Israel reacted to the presence of Palestinian gunmen with tanks, helicopter gunships, and rockets, ratcheting up the violence and responding with even stronger weaponry and military might.

The first intifada brought world attention to the plight of Palestinians and was in part responsible for creating the climate for the Oslo peace agreements. The second intifada made it nearly impossible for further peace to be achieved.

In 2001, the defeat of the Barak government led to the return of a familiar player on the political scene. Ariel Sharon was elected prime minister. The controversial, conservative leader of the Likud Party, whose career was once nearly extinguished in the disastrous aftermath of the 1982 War in Lebanon, had risen from the ashes and been elected leader of Israel. For the Palestinians, it sent a clear message that the man responsible for the death of hundreds, if not thousands, of Palestinians was now shaping Israeli politics. He was elected with a promise to achieve not peace, but security. These two aims require quite different actions, and Sharon made it clear that he would not hesitate to do what was necessary to ensure that his state was safe from attacks from outside—and inside—its borders.

And still representing the Palestinian cause, although weakened by the failure of his plan to achieve peace, is Yasir Arafat. A symbol of the struggle against Israel, he has most recently found himself in the awkward, if not impossible, position of trying to police the most violent and extreme elements of Palestinian freedom fighters, in effect trying to quell the violence against Israeli forces in a final attempt to achieve the aim for which he has fought so long—a Palestinian state.

His struggle to hold on to power has left the Palestinian cause with a figurehead who has symbolized the rights of a people left homeless. But at the same time, his inability to delegate power and to negotiate a successful resolution to the conflict has left the Palestinian movement splintered. In his absence, there are many more violent and extreme Palestinian leaders ready to take a very different approach to the conflict.

THE MYTH OF PEACE

Given the cycle of violence that has shaped the region for so many years, is it realistic to plan for peace? The personalities of Israeli, Arab, and Palestinian leaders have, in many ways, shaped the dialogue. With each new government, hope springs up once again that a solution may be reached, and that the violence and bloodshed may end.

But the issues upon which the conflict has been built are

many and difficult. Who are the rightful tenets of a patch of land? Those who claim to have received it from God in ancient times? Those who have worked it for hundreds of years? Those who have rightfully been granted it as the result of accords and agreements? Those who fought for it with blood and bullets?

A lasting peace would need to address the issue of Jewish settlements in the West Bank and Gaza. Should those who view themselves as pioneers, who have built a living in often-hostile territory, be now forced out? Or can the land be truly considered theirs if the presence of troops and armed guards is required for them to hold onto it?

How should the Gaza Strip be handled? It is one of the most densely populated places on the planet—a tiny patch of land onto which some 6,000 Jewish settlers and nearly a million Palestinians are crammed. The people here are poor, and the region is heavily dependent on Israel.

And what of Jerusalem? In many ways, this question put an end to the peace process attempted by Ehud Barak and Yasir Arafat. Jerusalem contains sites that are holy to Muslims, Jews, and Christians. In East Jerusalem is found The Temple Mount, where Jews believe that redemption (forgiveness of sins) will take place when the Messiah comes. To give up Jerusalem would in a sense mean giving up this critical element of their faith—the promise of redemption. The very same area is known as *Haram al-Sharif* (Noble Sanctuary) to Muslims, the place where, according to the Koran, the Prophet Muhammad rose up to heaven. How could this place be divided?

With questions like these unanswered, the prospects for peace seem bleak, indeed. What seems certain is that it will take courageous leaders on all sides who are willing to make concessions, and willing to rewrite history, if the Israeli and Arab peoples are to move away from the bitter

Jerusalem, one of the main issues in the Israel/Palestinian conflict, has religious meaning in both the Jewish and Muslim religions. It contains the Temple Mount, a site that holds the promise of redemption for Jews, and is also the site where the Prophet Muhammad, the founding figure of Islam, rose up to heaven. How can this city be divided between members of the two religions?

disputes of the past toward a bright, peaceful future.

For now, the state of Israel remains a nation still fighting for its freedom. The process begun in the Tel Aviv Museum on that long-ago day in May 1948 has resulted in an independent state, but its independence has been bought at a high price. Israel has carved out a home for Jews from the often-inhospitable land. But it has failed in the goal outlined in its declaration of independence—the goal of peaceful cooperation with the Arabs of Israel and neighboring Arab nations in a common effort to promote the advancement of the entire Middle East.

70 A.D. Roman Empire seizes Jerusalem; most Jewish residents of the region are sent into exile.

644 A.D. Palestine and surrounding region becomes Islamic territory.

1516 Palestine becomes part of the Ottoman Empire.

1882-1903 First large group of Jewish immigrants from Eastern Europe arrive in Palestine.

1909 Tel Aviv is established as the first Jewish city in Palestine.

1914-18 World War I takes place; Ottoman Empire (including Palestinian territory) sides with Germany against the Allies.

1920-48 British mandate in Palestine.

1942 Arab League is founded in Cairo, Egypt.

1947 Great Britain asks U.N. to help resolve crisis in Palestine. General assembly recommends partition of Palestine into two states. Civil war begins between Jews and Arabs in Palestine.

1948 British mandate ends. The state of Israel declares its independence. Armies from Egypt, Jordan, Syria, Lebanon, and Iraq attack Israel.

1949 Israel negotiates armistices with Egypt, Jordan, Lebanon, and Syria. Israel holds first parliamentary elections; David Ben-Gurion becomes first prime minister.

1950 Israeli government moves from Tel Aviv to Jerusalem.

1952 Egypt's King Farouk is overthrown following a revolution.

1956 Nasser nationalizes Suez Canal; Israel joins with Great Britain and France to plan invasion of Egypt to overthrow Nasser. Israel invades Sinai and Gaza.

1958 Civil war in Lebanon; revolution in Iraq.

1964 PLO is founded.

1967 Israel launches attack on Egypt, Syria, and Iraq. After cease-fire is declared, Israel occupies East Jerusalem, West Bank, Golan Heights, Sinai, and Gaza.

1969 PLO elects Yasir Arafat as chairman. Golda Meir becomes prime minister of Israel.

1973 Egypt and Syria attack Israel in start of Yom Kippur War (also known as Ramadan War or October War). Cease-fire declared 16 days after war begins. Arab nations begin oil embargo targeting the United States.

1974 U.N. general assembly recognizes PLO as official representative of Palestinian people and invites Arafat to speak.

1977 Likud Party wins Israeli elections; Begin becomes prime minister and launches expansion of Jewish settlements in West Bank.

1978 Camp David peace agreement is signed by Israel, Egypt, and United States.

1981 Israel bombs Iraqi nuclear reactor; Sadat is killed by Islamic militants.

1982 Israel invades Lebanon in Peace for Galilee operation.

1987 Palestinian Intifada begins.

1988 Jordan's King Hussein gives up claims to West Bank territory.

1990 Iraq invades Kuwait.

1991 Gulf War results in defeat of Iraq by U.N. coalition force.

1993 Secret Israel-PLO talks in Oslo, Norway begin.

1994 Beginning of limited Palestinian authority in Gaza and Jericho. Israel-Jordan peace treaty signed.

1995 Rabin and Arafat sign interim peace agreement in Washington, D.C. Rabin is assassinated.

1996 First Palestinian elections held; Arafat wins presidency. Netanyahu becomes Israeli prime minister.

1997 Hebron handed over to Palestinian control.

1999 Ehud Barak becomes prime minister.

2000 Barak, Arafat, and U.S. president Clinton meet at Camp David; are unable to reach an agreement for peace. Second Intifada begins in Palestine.

2001 Ariel Sharon becomes prime minister.

BOOKS:

Ben-Gurion, David. *Israel: A Personal History.* New York: Herzl Press, 1972.

Bregman, Ahron and El-Tahri, Jihan. *The Fifty Years' War: Israel and the Arabs.* New York: TV Books, 1998.

Friedman, Thomas L. *From Beirut to Jerusalem.* New York: Anchor Books, 1990.

Lewis, Bernard. *The Middle East: A Brief History of the Last 2,000 Years.* New York: Touchstone Books, 1997.

Meir, Golda. *My Life.* New York: G.P. Putnam's Sons, 1975.

Peretz, Don. *The Arab-Israel Dispute.* New York: Facts on File, 1996.

Tessler, Mark. *A History of the Israeli-Palestinian Conflict.* Bloomington: Indiana University Press, 1994.

Wallach, Janet and Wallach, John. *Arafat: In the Eyes of the Beholder.* New York: Carol Publishing Group, 1990.

WEB SITES:

www.arab.net

www.bbc.co.uk

www.britannica.com

www.idf.il

www.jordantimes.com

www.jpost.co.il

www.mfa.gov.il

www.pna.net

www.worldbookonline.com

HEATHER LEHR WAGNER is a writer and editor. She has an M.A. in government from the College of William and Mary and a B.A. in political science from Duke University. She is the author of two additional books on the Middle East—*Iraq* and *Turkey* in the Creation of the Modern Middle East series. She is also the author of *The IRA and England* in the People at Odds series.